WINDOWS XP

in easy steps

D1395725

HARSHAD KOTECHA

COMPUTER
STEP

In easy steps is an imprint of Computer Step
Southfield Road . Southam
Warwickshire CV47 0FB . England

http://www.ineasysteps.com

Notice of Liability
Every effort has been made to ensure that this book contains accurate and current information. However, Computer Step and the author shall not be liable for any loss or damage suffered by readers as a result of any information contained herein.

Trademarks
Microsoft® and Windows® are registered trademarks of Microsoft Corporation. All other trademarks are acknowledged as belonging to their respective companies.

Printed and bound in the United Kingdom

ISBN 1-84078-236-6

Contents

Managing Files and Folders 51

4

Working with Programs 73

5

The Internet and .NET Passport 89

6

Getting Started

This chapter explains what Windows is and what's new in this latest major upgrade. You will learn how to log on, switch to another user and shut down a Windows XP computer properly and safely. The new-look Desktop and Start menu are explained. Then, the extensive online help system is covered including how to get outside support if all else fails. Finally, the new Activation feature of Windows XP is explained.

Covers

Chapter One

What is Windows?

Windows is an *operating system*. This is the sofware that organises and controls all the components in your computer (both hardware and software) so that they integrate and work efficiently together. All computers need an operating system to function and Windows is the most popular one as it's installed on most of the world's PCs (personal computers).

The basic foundation underlying any version of Windows is its 'windowing' capability. A window (spelt with a lower-case w) is a rectangular area used to display information or to run a program. Several windows can be opened at the same time to work with multiple applications, so you should be able to dramatically increase your productivity when using your PC.

Windows XP (XP stands for eXPerience) is the latest version of Windows developed by Microsoft. It is the first version of Windows designed for both the consumer (Home Edition) and the business user (Professional). Windows XP Professional includes all the features of Windows XP Home Edition plus some advanced capabilities including enhanced networking, mobile computing, corporate management and security. This book covers both editions, catering for all Windows XP users.

What's New in Windows XP?

Here are ten major new features and improvements in Windows XP and perhaps the reasons you should be using it:

1 **New Sleek Look.** Windows XP has been completely redesigned visually so that it's more intuitive and simple. The brand new task-oriented design helps you get to where you want to, straightaway.

2 **Reliability.** Many users will upgrade to Windows XP just for this single feature – thanks to its new engine providing stability. In the past, installing applications or drivers for new hardware devices made Windows unstable. Now, Windows XP protects key system files from being overwritten and therefore dramatically reducing system-crashes.

Windows XP has a new engine that makes it the most reliable version of Windows so far.

3 **Ease of Use.** Starting from the new Welcome screen providing easy access to your computer, Windows XP offers many other features that makes it a lot easier to use. You'll see these features throughout this book.

4 **Performance.** Windows XP is much faster than before. One of the ways it achieves better performance is by intelligent pre-fetching of files during boot-up and usage. It learns which files are always required when you start your computer and makes them available in fast cache memory before you need them. Windows XP becomes over 90% optimised after about three reboots or three days from installation. It also reserves more space for your applications.

5 **Enhanced Internet Experience.** Windows XP makes the web faster, more secure, and easier to use. It's based on the new Internet Explorer 6 browser with enhanced toolbars and buttons.

6 **Digital Media.** You'll be able to easily share and enjoy photos, home videos and music on your PC.

If you're spending a lot of time in front of your screen, ClearType will make it a lot less tiring on your eyes.

7 **Mobility.** For laptop users Windows XP provides better power management so your battery life is extended, you can use two monitors off a single display adapter – ideal for presentations. Also, the new ClearType technology used smooths the text display to increase screen readability.

8 **Communications.** This includes straightforward setting up of a network; improved Windows Messenger (used for sending instant messages) which now also integrates voice and video to text communication (provided you have the necessary hardware); Remote Desktop (Professional edition only) allows you to access your work machine from your home computer; and you can set up wireless connection to other devices like the new Pocket PC 2002.

9 **Security and Privacy.** Includes Internet Connection Firewall, personalised Login and File Encryption.

10 **Improved Help and Support.** This centres around Windows XP's own online Help and Support Center.

Using your Mouse

Scroll More Easily

Zoom Efficiently

Raised Back Fits Your Hand

The wheel only works in software that has been specifically designed for it, like Microsoft Windows, Internet Explorer and Office.

A mouse is a pointing device used to communicate with your computer. The Microsoft IntelliMouse (as shown above) includes the standard two buttons plus a wheel sited between them. Use your index finger to operate the small wheel. This provides an extra level of speed and control when scrolling up and down documents or even web pages - it's much faster than clicking on the scroll arrows displayed. You can even use the wheel to zoom into images and text.

To use a mouse, first place it on a flat surface or a mouse mat. You will notice an arrow-headed pointer ( ) moving on your screen as you move the mouse.

To make a selection, move the mouse pointer on top of an item and then press and release (or click) the left mouse button. Sometimes you can click twice in rapid succession (double-click) to open a folder, window, or a program.

You can set Windows to accept a single-click instead of the default double-click. See page 48 for further details.

A mouse will usually have at least one more button on the right (called the right mouse button). This provides further facilities – for example, a right-click of the mouse button when it is over an appropriate object will display a shortcut menu of related options for further selection.

A mouse can also be used to move items on the screen. This is achieved by first moving the mouse pointer over an item. Then, press and hold down the left mouse button and move the mouse to position the item. Finally, once you see the item in the new location, release the mouse button. This technique is called 'dragging'.

In this guide we will use the terms: Click, Double-click, Right-click and Drag to refer to mouse operations described above.

Starting Windows XP

After you switch on your computer the Welcome screen will be displayed. Here, click on your user name/picture to gain access to your own Windows computer. If set up, you may also be asked to type your password. Simply type it in and press the Enter key or click here.

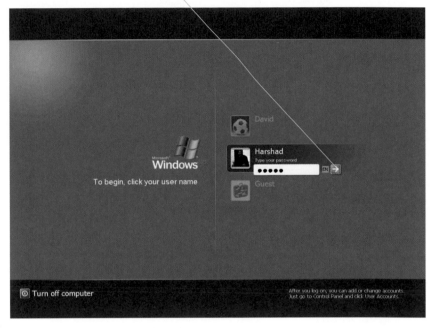

Set up new users and change their settings, including setting up a Guest account and changing the picture associated with the user name (to their own photo for example) – see page 143.

If multiple users are set up to use and share the same PC, then it's easy to switch between them. Each user can create a separate password-protected (optional) account with his/her own personalised desktop and settings.

Several accounts can be active at the same time – you don't need to close your programs and log off to be able to switch to another user. All your settings and files are maintained but the new user won't be able to see them; and you won't be able to see theirs when you switch back. Your screen will look exactly the same as you left it.

To switch users, click on the Start button, Log Off, Switch User. Alternatively, for **Fast-User Switching** just press the Windows key+L.

The Desktop

Your desktop may look different, depending on the Windows components and software you have installed, and any customisation that has been done.

Instructions in this book tell you to double-click on icons to launch the associated programs (the default).

However, you can change this to accept a single-click to open an item. See page 48, Folder Options, for how to achieve this.

If you have not upgraded from a previous installation, your Windows XP desktop should not have any *icons* except the Recycle Bin. As a result, most of the desktop is a tidy blank area.

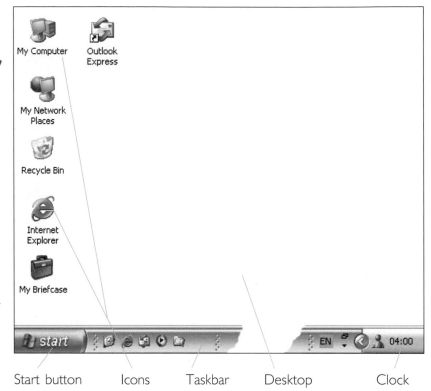

Start button   Icons   Taskbar   Desktop   Clock

Double-click on icons to start the tasks they represent – you can create your own shortcut icons for frequent programs that you'll be using – see page 77.

Single-click the Start button to access your programs, files, change settings, get help and turn off your computer (see the next page).

The *taskbar* at the bottom (by default) can be moved to any of the other edges of the desktop (see page 150). A *task button* is created on here automatically for every program running – click on it to switch between them (see page 29 and 80).

The Start Button

The Start button on the taskbar is revamped for the better. As well as providing access to all the items if required, the main display only shows the most frequently used programs and files. The idea is that you're likely to want to work with one of these and therefore it avoids unnecessary clutter.

These are fixed or "pinned" items that are always there so you can launch them quickly.

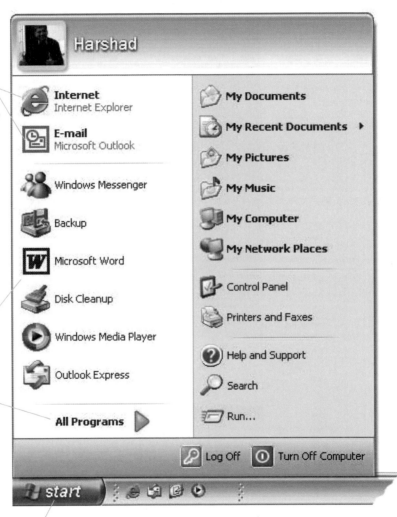

These change with links to the programs you use most frequently.

Place you mouse pointer over All Programs to access all your installed programs.

Click on the Start button. From here you can do almost everything: Start programs, Access your files, Customise your settings from the Control Panel, get Help and Support, Search for items on your computer or the Internet, and much more.

Online Help

Right-clicking on many options, buttons and areas of Windows XP screens will display a short menu labelled 'What's This?'. Click on this to display a short explanation or definition of the item on the screen.

Click anywhere to close the explanation box.

The Windows XP Help system has been completely redesigned. Choose Help and Support from the Start button, or click on the Help menu from any folder and then select Help and Support Center.

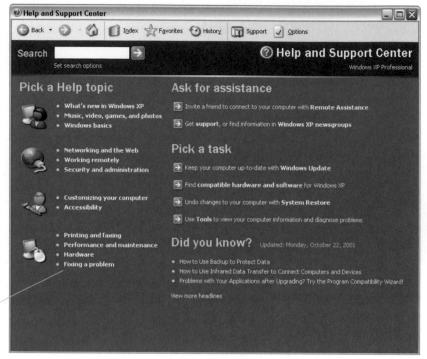

Click on 'Fixing a problem' to help you diagnose and fix technical problems.

Click on any topic you want help on.

2 Select the topic you want help on from the left pane.

Your desktop icons

Pick a task:

Arrange your desktop icons

Rename a desktop icon

Turn off the desktop icon grid

Remove unused desktop icons

3 If a topic is further divided into tasks, click on the appropriate one from the right pane to display the specific Help information.

Click here to display just the specific Help text

Click here to get a printout of the specific Help text

Use the Back and Forward browser buttons to navigate through your help pages.

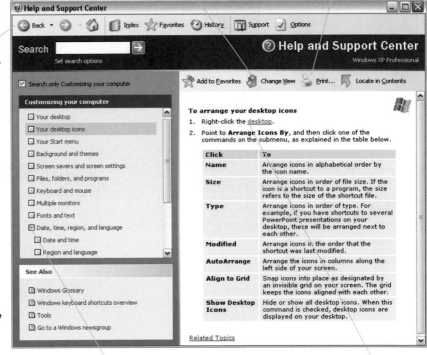

Topics prefixed with a Question mark icons (?) contain actual help information.

Click on the plus icon (+) to expand a topic or on minus (-) to collapse grouped help topics

Click on underlined (hyperlink) text for further help/definition

4 Click on the Close (X) button when you have finished.

Using the Help Index

To find specific help on how to do something in Windows XP use the Index. All topics are listed in alphabetical order here so you can find related ones easily by scrolling up or down.

| Open the Help and Support Center as described on page 14.

2 Click on the Index button.

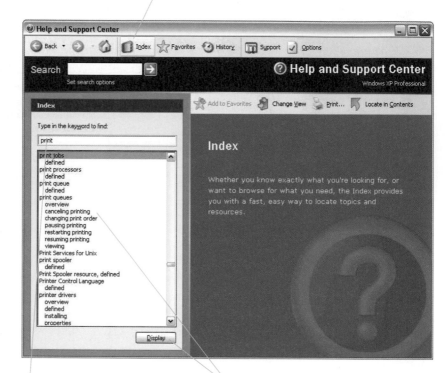

Re step 4: Sometimes a further selection window appears before the Help is displayed.

3 Type in the key letters of the word(s) you want help on. The index will automatically scroll to the start of the topics beginning with the text you typed.

4 Click on the appropriate matching topic and then the Display button (or just double-click the topic to save time) and the relevant help appears in the right window pane.

Using the Search Box

If you don't find the topic you're looking for in the Index, type in a phrase in the Search box.

1   Open the Help and Support Center as described on page 14.

2   Type in your phrase here.

Click here to customise the way the search works and the way results are displayed.

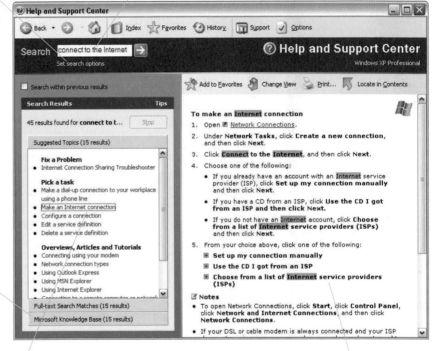

Click on the Microsoft Knowledge Base button to display links to online articles published relating to your search query.

Type "walk-throughs" in the Search box to find overviews, articles and tutorials on some of the main features.

3   Click on the desired task.

4   The Help for it is displayed here, with any key words in your Search box highlighted.

5   Click on the shortcut icon ▣ (or the related underlined text) to display the referenced dialog box and alter the settings rightaway as you're reading about it.

Assisted Support

If you can't solve your problem by using the self-help features discussed in the previous four pages, then you need further assistance. There are two main ways you can get this:

1. Remote Assistance

This is a new approach based on the premise that it's likely that your friend or work colleague is likely to have had the same problems as you've been experiencing. Therefore, with your permisssion, they can access your system and see your desktop in the hope that they'll be able to help. You can even give this control to a company offering support services. For Remote Assistance to work both parties must be running Windows XP.

You must only share control of your system with an individual or company you really trust.

If you get nervous at any stage, just press the ESC key to terminate the Remote Assistance.

Click on Support and then 'Ask a friend to help' from the left pane.

Click on the Home button to display the main Help and Support Center page at any time (as shown on page 14).

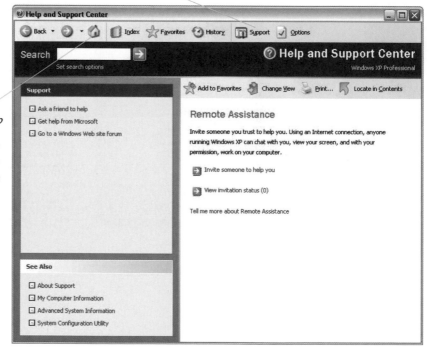

2 Click on 'Invite someone to help you' and then choose how you want to contact your assistant: via Windows Messenger or email (both covered in Chapter 7).

Visit these websites for other technical information and help:

www.microsoft.com/ windowsxp/expertzone/ articlelinks.asp

www.microsoft.com/ windowsxp/expertzone/ relatedsites.asp

www.microsoft.com/ windowsxp/expertzone/ newsgroups/default.asp

www.microsoft.com/uk/ support/self_support.asp

2. Microsoft Online Assisted Support (OAS)

This allows you to contact a Microsoft Support Professional via the Internet. You'll need to submit all the relevant information in what is known as an 'Electronic Support Incident' to enable Microsoft to understand your problem and provide a solution.

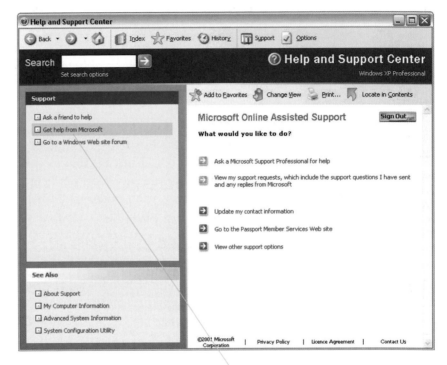

1 Click on Support and then 'Get help from Microsoft' from the left pane.

2 Sign in using your .NET passport (see page 104 on how to create this). Microsoft have already registered all Hotmail and MSN email accounts as Passports so, if you have one, you can use that instead.

3 Click on 'Ask a Microsoft Support Professional for help'.

Product Activation

Microsoft Product Activation is a new Windows XP feature. Its purpose is to reduce software piracy and to ensure that a licensed version of the software can only be used on one PC.

Activation shouldn't be confused with Registration. It works by checking that the unique software product key (the combination of letters and numbers on the CD's case), which you'll need to enter when installing the software, hasn't been used on more than one PC.

You'll not be able to install your single-user Windows XP software on your work PC as well as your home PC – even though you can only use one computer at any one time – you'll have to buy a new copy/license.

Activation takes under a minute to complete over the Internet and, unlike registration, no personal details are collected. If you don't have Internet access you can choose to complete the activation over the phone. You'll have 30 days to activate Windows XP after first installing it. If you don't activate it within this time then you'll not be able to continue using Windows until you do activate it. Windows keeps track of your 30 days grace period and often pops up a reminder in the *notification area* – this is on the taskbar opposite to the Start button.

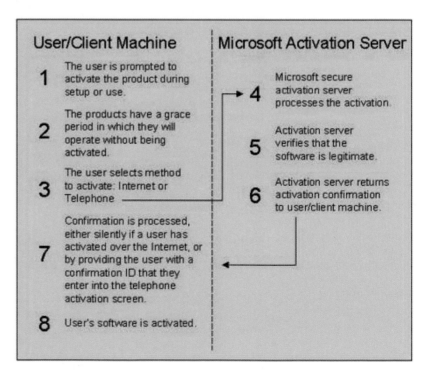

User/Client Machine	Microsoft Activation Server
1 The user is prompted to activate the product during setup or use.	4 Microsoft secure activation server processes the activation.
2 The products have a grace period in which they will operate without being activated.	5 Activation server verifies that the software is legitimate.
3 The user selects method to activate: Internet or Telephone	6 Activation server returns activation confirmation to user/client machine.
7 Confirmation is processed, either silently if a user has activated over the Internet, or by providing the user with a confirmation ID that they enter into the telephone activation screen.	
8 User's software is activated.	

Log Off/Turn Off your Computer

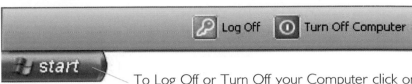

To Log Off or Turn Off your Computer click on the Start button to reveal both options at the bottom of the Start menu.

If you turn off the power switch without following the steps here you could corrupt important files and lose valuable information.

Log Off option

Click on this option if you have temporarily finished using your computer. Windows will then display this screen:

Switch User – click here if someone else wants to use your computer for a few minutes. The Welcome screen is displayed, from which a new user can log on. Any programs and documents you had open are kept in exactly the same state, so when you switch back the display is exactly as you left it.

Once you've logged off, you can use the Turn Off Computer button on the Welcome screen to shut down.

Log Off – click here to save your work and return to the Welcome screen. From here, you/another user can log on again.

Turn Off Computer option

Choose this option from the Start menu at the end of the day or when no one will be using the computer. Windows presents you with the final Turn off computer window:

Stand By – this is to conserve power. Windows XP turns off your monitor and hard disks but keeps all the programs currently running in memory open. It doesn't save your work automatically, so you should save your work before using this option. Then, press any key or move the mouse to wake up your computer for normal use.

Turn Off – click here and Windows XP saves any unsaved work before turning off your computer. Most newer-type monitors are also turned off automatically.

Restart – this also saves your work and shuts down your computer, but it starts it up again rightaway. Click on this option after making changes to some of your Windows settings and you want these to take effect, or after installing some programs.

Hibernate – only appears on some computers. If you don't see it initially, hold down the Shift key and the Stand By button is replaced by the Hibernate button. Its function is similar to the Stand By mode, but it also saves whatever's in memory at the time to your hard disk. So when you turn your PC back on, the memory state is loaded automatically and your desktop and open programs appear just as you left them – you can then simply carry on from the point you left off. The Hibernate mode is not as safe as the Turn Off option so try and avoid using it.

If your computer freezes or one of your applications locks up, press Ctrl+Alt+Del keys to bring up Windows Task Manager (see page 81) – from here you can close the application, log off a user or shut down Windows.

Basic Controls

Most of what you do in Windows XP will be done using a menu, dialog box or a window. This chapter shows you how you can use these structures.

Covers

Chapter Two

Menus

Most of the windows will have a Menu bar near the top, displaying the menu options relevant to a particular window. Simply click on a menu option to reveal a drop-down list of further options within it. As an example, we will look at the View menu from My Computer window:

A forward arrow indicates that there is another linked menu for selection. Move the mouse arrow onto the option to see it.

A tick shows that an option is active.

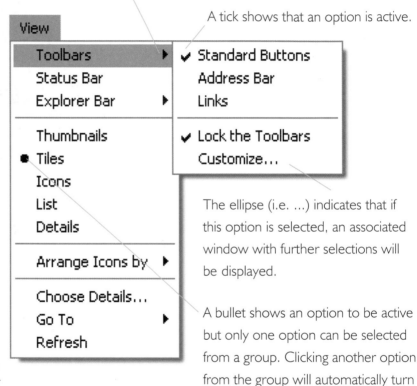

The ellipse (i.e. ...) indicates that if this option is selected, an associated window with further selections will be displayed.

A bullet shows an option to be active but only one option can be selected from a group. Clicking another option from the group will automatically turn off the previously selected one.

Some examples of shortcut keys are:

Ctrl+Z – Undo
Ctrl+X – Cut
Ctrl+C – Copy
Ctrl+V – Paste
Ctrl+A – Select All

To deactivate an option with a tick next to it, click on it. Click on it again to activate it. If an option is dimmed out, it cannot be used at that particular time or is not appropriate. Some options may have shortcut keys next to them so you can use these instead of clicking on them with your mouse.

Dialog boxes

Although simple settings can be made quickly from menu options, other settings need to be made from windows displayed specifically for this purpose. These are called dialog boxes.

Tabs

Click on the appropriate one to display its settings.

Check boxes

Click on as many as required. A tick indicates that the option is active. If you click on it again it will be turned off. If an option is dimmed out, it cannot be selected.

Radio buttons

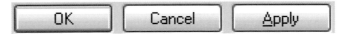

Only one out of a group of radio buttons can be selected. If you click on another radio button, the previously selected one is automatically turned off.

Action buttons

OK will save the settings selected and close the dialog box or window. Cancel will close the window without saving the amended settings – click on it if you've made a mistake. Apply will save the settings selected so far but will not close the window, in case you want to make further changes.

Structure of a window

Dialog boxes are usually fixed-size windows and therefore don't have scroll bars, minimise, maximise, restore buttons or the control icon. They also don't display resize pointers at the edges.

All windows are similar in their structure. You can have a window containing icons for further selection, or a window that displays a screen from a program.

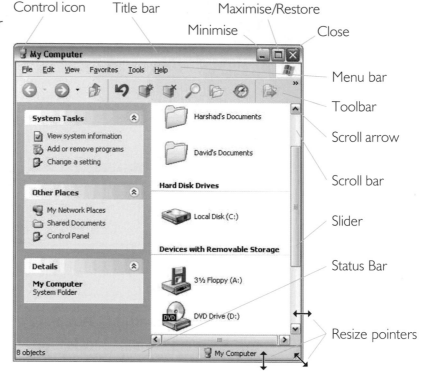

Control icon   Title bar   Maximise/Restore
Minimise   Close
Menu bar
Toolbar
Scroll arrow
Scroll bar
Slider
Status Bar
Resize pointers

To hide the Status Bar, click on Status Bar from the View menu.

Double-click on an icon to open a window relating to it.

From the View menu, click on Toolbars and then select to display other toolbars (Address, Links) or deselect existing ones.

The Status Bar displays information about items selected from the window. The scroll bars will only appear when (as here) there are items that cannot fit into the current size of the window.

If you move the mouse pointer over any edge of a window, the pointer changes shape and becomes a double-headed resize pointer – drag it to change the size of a window (see page 30 – Resizing a window).

Moving a window

As long as a window is not maximised, occupying the whole screen, you can move it. This is especially useful if you have several windows open and need to organise your desktop.

1 Move the mouse pointer over the Title bar of a window.

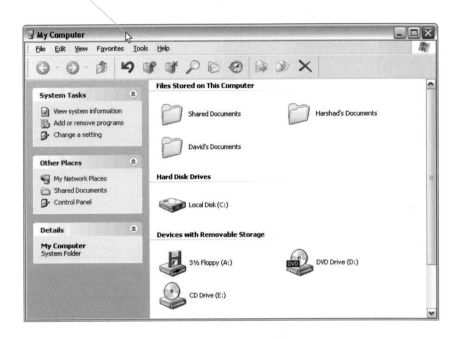

2 Drag the mouse pointer to a new location.

3 When the window is in the desired location, release the mouse button.

Maximising, Minimising and Restoring a window

A window can be maximised to fill the whole screen, minimised to a button on the Taskbar, or restored to the original size.

You can also double-click on the Title bar to maximise the window.

Maximised window   Minimise button   Restore button

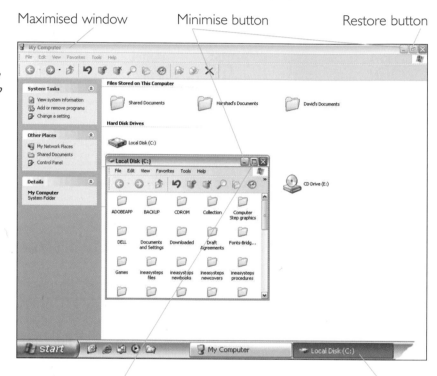

Maximise button   Task button

Click the Control icon (top left) or right-click the task button, to display a shortcut menu that also allows you to minimise, maximise and restore the window.

Whether a window is maximised or the original size, click on the minimise button (left of the top-right three buttons) to reduce the window to a Task button. This will create space on the desktop for you to work in other windows. When you want to restore the reduced window, simply click on it from the Taskbar.

The middle button (out of the three) can either be a maximise button, or – if the window is already maximised – the same button changes to a restore button.

Switching between windows/tasks

Switching between windows cannot be easier. The task (window) that is active has its title bar, menu bar and outside window frame highlighted. If you have more than one window displayed on the desktop, click anywhere inside a window that is not active to activate it or switch to it.

 If you have too many windows open so that their task buttons don't fit on the taskbar, then task buttons become grouped automatically by the task or program that created them:

Taskbar grouping is a new feature in Windows XP – see page 80 for further details.

 Press the Alt+Tab keys to toggle and switch between tasks.

active task button   active window

Another method of 'task switching' is to use the taskbar at the bottom. Every window that is open has a button created automatically on the taskbar. Therefore, it does not matter if the window you want to switch to is overlaid with others and you cannot see it. Just click on the button for it in the taskbar and the window will appear on top and it will be active.

Resizing a window

If a window is not maximised or minimised, it can be resized.

Resize and move windows on your desktop to the way you prefer to work.

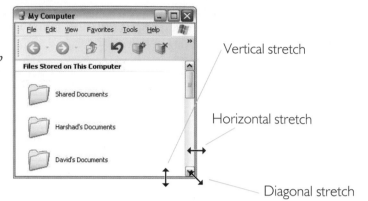

Vertical stretch

Horizontal stretch

Diagonal stretch

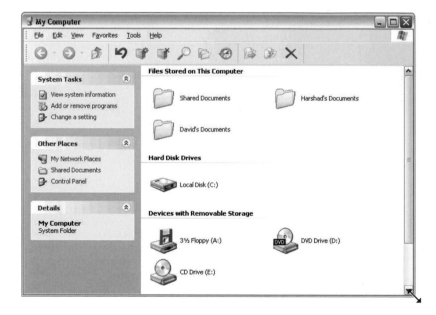

Place the mouse arrow anywhere on the edge of a window. It will change to a double-headed resize pointer.

2 Drag the pointer outwards to increase the size of the window, or inwards to reduce the size. Release the mouse button when the window is the desired size.

Arranging windows

If you have several windows open on your desktop and you want to automatically rearrange them neatly, rather than resize and move each one individually, use the Cascade or Tile options.

To get rid of the clutter quickly, choose Show the Desktop from the taskbar shortcut menu.

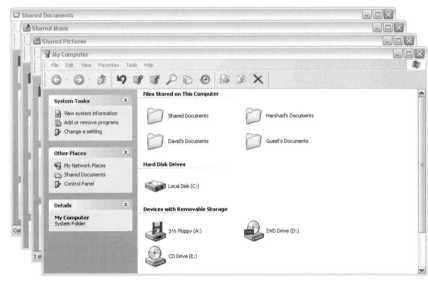

Click on Undo... (where the dots represent the original command) to restore your windows to how they were before you rearranged them.

If you have a grouped task button (see page 29), right-click on it to Cascade or Tile the windows it contains.

Right-click on the taskbar to display a shortcut menu.

Click on Cascade Windows (overlaps all the windows so that just the Title bars are visible, except for the front one), Tile Windows Horizontally (resizes each window equally and displays them across the screen in rows), or Tile Windows Vertically (resizes each window equally and displays them across the screen in columns).

Arranging icons

If you have icons displayed in a folder (View menu, Icons), you can rearrange the order in many different ways. The example here shows you how to organise your desktop icons.

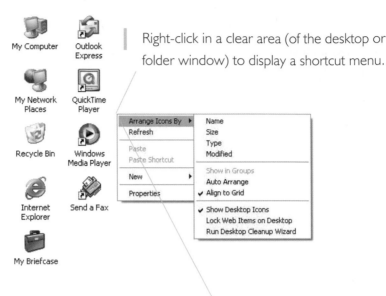

1 Right-click in a clear area (of the desktop or folder window) to display a shortcut menu.

2 Move the pointer over **Arrange Icons By** to reveal another menu.

You can drag an icon out of the window and onto the desktop or another window.

3 Click on an option to arrange all the icons in a preferred sequence (**Name**, **Size**, **Type**, **Modified**). If Auto Arrange is deselected, you can manually arrange all your icons by simply dragging them into position. **Align to Grid** snaps icons to an invisible grid and so forces them to be aligned with each other. Select **Auto Arrange** to neatly arrange all the icons in columns along the left.

Show in Groups option

You'll be able to select the new Show in Groups option from all folders, but not the Desktop. This groups your files and folders alphabetically by name, size, type, etc. See page 43 for further details.

Scrolling

If a window is not big enough to display all the information within it, then a Scroll bar will appear automatically. Use it to see the contents of a window not immediately in view.

The size of the Slider in relation to the Scroll bar indicates how much of the total contents are in view. The position tells you which portion is in view.

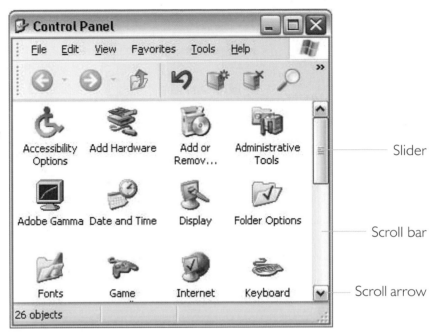

Slider

Scroll bar

Scroll arrow

1 Drag the Slider along the Scroll bar towards one of the two Scroll arrows to scroll in that direction.

or

2 Click on the Scroll bar to display the next window's amount of information towards the Scroll arrow nearest to it.

or

3 Click on one of the Scroll arrows to scroll just a little in that direction. Hold down your mouse button to scroll continuously.

Closing a window

When you've finished with a window you will need to close it. There are several ways of doing this – use the method that's easiest and the most appropriate at the time.

Save your work before closing any program window in which you've been working.

Click on the Close button (top right corner).

If Minimised

Right click on the minimised task button.

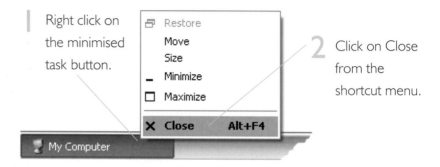

2 Click on Close from the shortcut menu.

From the Control icon

Click on the Control icon (top left corner).

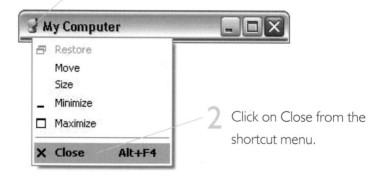

2 Click on Close from the shortcut menu.

From the keyboard

Press Alt+F4 to close the active window.

My Computer and Windows Explorer

The easiest way to access or browse all the information on your computer is via My Computer. However, you can use Windows Explorer instead, which is very similar; hence they are both covered together in this chapter.

You'll also learn that the way you access information on your computer is very similar to accessing any external information from the Internet/web and other computers that you may be networked to.

Covers

Chapter Three

My Computer

One way to look for any of your files, regardless of where they are stored, involves using My Computer. Select it from the Start menu (click on the Start button and then click on My Computer from the right pane), or double-click on the My Computer icon from the desktop, if present.

My Computer

Select My Computer to open its window.

files in shared and user
documents folders

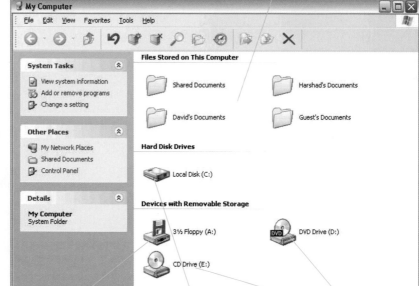

This computer has a DVD drive (D:) and a writable CD drive (E:).

files in your
floppy disk drive

files in your
main hard disk

files in your DVD/
CD-ROM drives

2 Double-click on the appropriate drive icon (ensuring that you have first inserted a floppy disk/CD/DVD) or folder to display files/folders it contains.

Context Sensitive Task Panes

This is a new feature in Windows XP and it's very useful. On the left hand side of a folder window you'll see a series of panels called *task panes*. This is the default view from My Computer.

A File is a basic unit of storage. All your programs and documents (including pictures, music, videos) are stored as files.

A Folder is used to group related files together. A folder may contain files and other folders.

If the window is too small to display all task panes, click here to collapse a particular one, so that another more relevant task pane is brought into view.

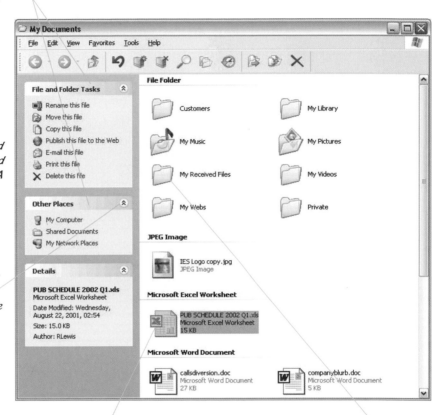

File   Folder

If My Pictures folder is displayed, the Picture Tasks pane is shown with options to View as a slide show, Order prints online, etc... My Music folder brings up Music tasks, and so on.

The task panes displayed will depend on the type of information you have in the right pane. Furthermore, depending on what you select from the right pane, the relevant options will appear in the task panes for you to select from – hence the term "context-sensitive". For example, if you click on a file, its details appear in the Details task pane and also options like Rename this file, Move this file, ... appear in the File and Folder Tasks pane (as shown above). If you clicked on a DVD/CD drive icon (last page) you'll see an option to Eject this disk.

Windows Explorer

Another way to display the files and folders on your computer is to use Windows Explorer.

Starting Windows Explorer

1 Click on the Start button, move your mouse pointer to All Programs, then Accessories and click on Windows Explorer.

or

2 Right-click on My Computer icon and then click on Explore from the shortcut menu displayed.

You can extend this to any folder icon displayed anywhere in Windows to display the Windows Explorer view with the contents of the selected folder on display in the right pane by default.

or

3 Right-click on the Start button and then click on Explore in the shortcut menu to display the contents of the Start menu folder.

or

4 Click on any folder icon to select it, then click on the File menu and select the Explore option.

Windows Explorer display

From the default My Computer view of Task panes, click on the Folders button (to activate it) and display this view.

Folders view is the default Windows Explorer view. However, if you click on the Folders button (to deactivate it) the default My Computer view, with task panes on the left is displayed – as shown on page 37.

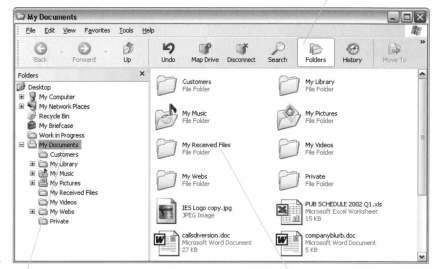

If you don't see the Standard buttons toolbar to be able to use the Folders button, activate it from the View menu, Toolbars.

1 Click on a folder you want to see the contents of. Folders and the files they contain are displayed on the right side. If you can't see all the folders, click on a plus sign to see the other folders it contains:

2 Double-click a program icon to start it, or a document/folder icon to open it.

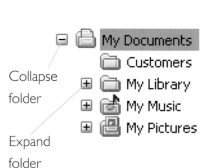

Collapse folder

Expand folder

Explorer Bar

The Folders view, as seen on the previous page, is part of the Explorer bar. This is the most popular view because it displays a structured hierarchy of all your drives and folders in the left pane. You'll also see in the next chapter how this view is useful to manage all your files. However, the Explorer bar can also display Search, Favorites, Media or History views (covered in Chapter 6). Select other views from the View menu, Explorer Bar or the appropriate button in Standard Buttons toolbar.

You can customise the Standard Buttons toolbar to show the buttons you want to see – see page 44.

Altering the split between panes

You may want to split the space between the two panes to control how much is displayed in each pane without scrolling or resizing the window.

Explorer Bar view name

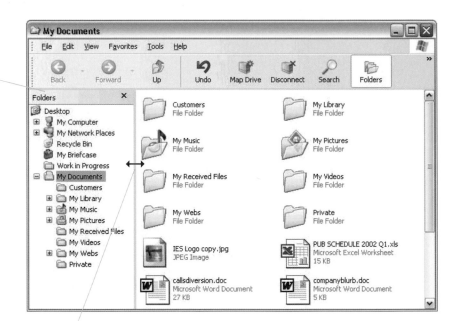

1 Move the mouse pointer over the border so that it changes to a double-headed arrow.

2 Drag the border towards left or right, as appropriate.

Changing the Display

Whether you are using My Computer or Windows Explorer, you can change the display of files from the View menu.

1 Click on the View menu option.

HOT TIP

Thumbnails are small representations of your picture graphics so you can see lots of them in one window.

2 Click on one of the display options. If you're displaying files from the Pictures folder, you'll also have the Filmstrip option (see page 154).

This is an example from Tiles view.

Sorting your Files

Windows allows you to sort your files in any drive or folder by any attribute or field like Name, Type, Size, Date Modified.

1 Click on the View menu option.

It's very useful to sort your files by Date Modified if you have several versions of the same file.

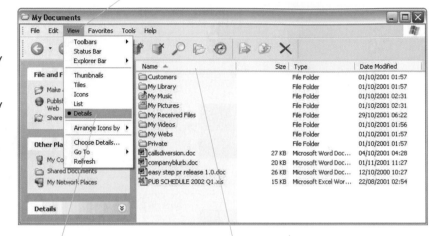

2 Select the Details display option.

3 Click on any column heading to sort the list by that attribute, or click on it again to sort it in reverse order.

The column that you have sorted will always display a little arrow in the heading representing the sort order: ▲ for ascending (lowest to highest) and ▼ for descending (highest to lowest).

The sorted column also has a lightly-tinted background to distinguish it from the other columns.

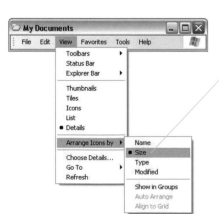

You can also sort by clicking on View, Arrange Icons by, and then selecting an attribute to sort by.

Show in Groups sort

If you have the Show in Groups display active (View, Arrange Icons by, Show in Groups selected/ticked), then your list will be sorted in groups. For example, if sorted by Size your files will be grouped into Tiny, Small, Medium, Large, Huge. A sort by date is shown below:

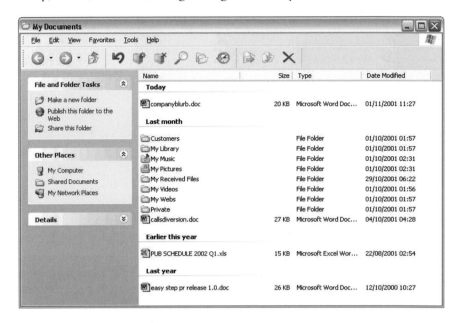

You decide on the Details displayed and sorted

You're not stuck with the default attributes shown in the Details view. Click on View, Choose Details... to display the Choose Details dialog box. Then, click to put a tick in the check boxes for attributes you want appearing (and also to deselect).

Change the order the attributes are displayed by selecting them and using the Move Up and Move Down buttons.

The Standard Buttons Toolbar

Windows XP provides Standard Buttons, Address Bar and Links toolbars from My Computer, Windows Explorer and other folders.

There are other toolbars displayed on the taskbar –

see page 150.

This is the most commonly used toolbar. If it's not already displayed select it from View, Toolbars. The Standard Buttons option should be ticked.

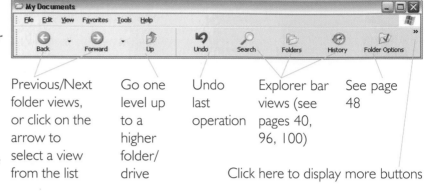

Previous/Next folder views, or click on the arrow to select a view from the list

Go one level up to a higher folder/drive

Undo last operation

Explorer bar views (see pages 40, 96, 100)

See page 48

Click here to display more buttons

Shortcut key: Press Backspace to see the higher level folder/drive.

Customise this toolbar to Move Up the buttons you use most. Disabling text labels and choosing small icons will allow more buttons to be displayed.

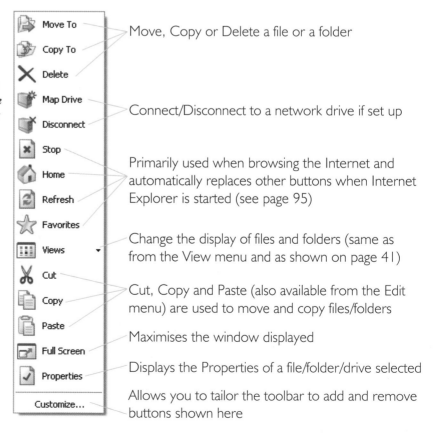

Move, Copy or Delete a file or a folder

Connect/Disconnect to a network drive if set up

Primarily used when browsing the Internet and automatically replaces other buttons when Internet Explorer is started (see page 95)

Change the display of files and folders (same as from the View menu and as shown on page 41)

Cut, Copy and Paste (also available from the Edit menu) are used to move and copy files/folders

Maximises the window displayed

Displays the Properties of a file/folder/drive selected

Allows you to tailor the toolbar to add and remove buttons shown here

The Address Bar

The Address Bar allows you to select and display contents from the main drives and folders in your system as well as from the Internet. Select it from View, Toolbars, so that the Address Bar option is ticked.

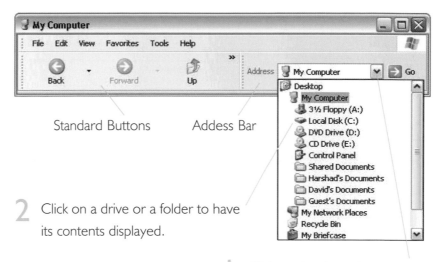

Standard Buttons   Addess Bar

2 Click on a drive or a folder to have its contents displayed.

Click on the drop-down arrow.

You'll notice that when you access the Internet, some Standard Buttons will be replaced to more appropriate ones for browsing the web.

You can type in any Internet web address here and then press the Enter key or click the Go button, or start typing the first bit of it and select a recently accessed site from the drop-down list

You can also access network drives from the Address Bar if your computer is connected to a network.

This is a very powerful feature! One minute you could be looking at a file in your computer and the next minute you could be accessing a web page on a computer on the other side of the globe – all from your same folder window.

The Links Toolbar

The Links toolbar provides shortcuts to major world wide web sites, without having to start your Internet Explorer browser program. To display the Links toolbar, click on View, Toolbars, and tick the Links option.

The Address and Links toolbars can also be displayed on the taskbar – see page 150.

click on a web address link

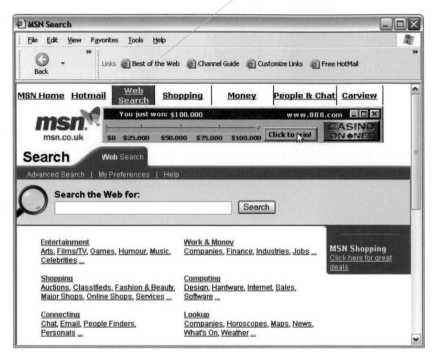

Customising the Links bar

This could not be simpler:

To add a shortcut to the Links bar, drag a web page's icon directly from the Address bar, or drag a link from any web page displayed, or from the Favorites bar (see page 98), or even the desktop.

To rearrange a shortcut on the Links bar, just drag it to the new position. To remove it from the Links bar, right-click on it to display a short menu and then choose Delete; and to change its icon, choose Properties from the short menu and then click on the Change Icon button.

Toolbar Sharing

It is possible to have all your toolbars active at the same time. However, just because you can do something, doesn't mean that you always should. The best approach is to activate the toolbars relevant to the tasks you are performing. If you need to have more than one toolbar active, then here's how you can share the space:

drag the vertical line to control how much of a toolbar is displayed in preference to others occupying the same space

Right-click at the start of any toolbar to display or turn off any of the toolbars.

double-click on a toolbar label to expand it to the maximum size that will fit and double-click on it again to minimise it to just the label showing

If you've found an ideal way to display your toolbars for the tasks you perform regularly, and you don't want them altered, then choose Lock the Toolbars option from either right-clicking on any one toolbar or from the View menu, Toolbars.

drag a toolbar above or below any other, or drag it onto another toolbar to share its space including with the menu bar at the top

Folder Options

You can set Windows XP to view folders in different ways, from My Computer and other places.

You can also select the Folder Options icon from the Control Panel.

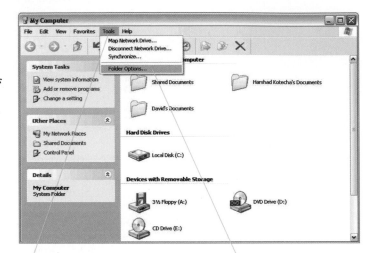

Click on the Tools menu.	2 Click on Folder Options...

You can combine different options to create a Windows environment you prefer.

3 Click on the options required (see next page).

4 Click OK to saves the changes made.

Tasks

The default is 'Show common tasks in folders'. This will provide you with context-sensitive task panes as described on page 37. Click on 'Use Windows classic folders' option to disable this and revert to folder views pre-Windows XP.

Browse folders

By default when you have one folder window displayed and you open another folder the contents of the new folder are displayed in the same window. This is fine for most uses but sometimes it's useful to have the contents of a new folder display in a new window. For example, for when you need to move or copy files between open folders.

If you open each folder in its own window, your desktop may soon be cluttered with windows you don't need.

Click on the Show Desktop icon (from the Quick Launch toolbar next to the Start button), to hide all the open windows on your desktop.

Click items as follows

The norm is to double-click an item with your mouse button to open it and single-click to select it. However, you may want to customize Windows to be consistent with the way you use the web, clicking once to open/hyperlink to an item.

Customizing Folders

You can customize the way your folders look graphically in Windows XP to help identify their contents.

1 Right-click on any folder icon, select Properties, and then the Customize tab.

You cannot customize My Documents, My Pictures, and My Music folders. However, you can customize other folders they may contain.

2 Select the options required: folder template (e.g. Pictures, Photo Album, etc), folder pictures (to choose a picture for your folder), folder icons (to change the folder icon).

3 Folder pictures are shown in Thumbnails view and your chosen folder icon in all other views.

Managing Files and Folders

Remember that folders are just logical names where files are stored. Windows XP handles operations (like moving, copying, deleting, etc.) on files and folders in a similar way and so they are both covered together here.

Covers

Chapter Four

Selecting Multiple Files/Folders

To select a single file or folder you simply click on it to highlight it. Then you can move, copy or delete it (see the next topic). However, if you want to perform these operations on several files or folders you'll need to select all of them, so that they can then be manipulated efficiently, in one fell swoop.

Adjacent block of files

To de-select all files, click once anywhere outside the selection area.

Selecting files here can include whole folders, which may contain other files.

| Drag out a box to cover all the files you want selected.

or

2 Click on the first item to select it. Then press and hold down the SHIFT key and click on the last item in the same group to highlight the whole group, indicating that it's selected.

Non-adjacent files

To de-select a file, Ctrl+click on it again.

Press Ctrl+A to select all files and folders in the active window.

To select several non-adjacent files, press and hold down the Ctrl key. Then click on as many files as required. If they're highlighted they're selected.

To select all files (and folders) in a window, click on Select All from the Edit menu.

Copying and Moving Files/Folders

You may want to copy/move a file to the same drive (a different folder) or to another (CD/floppy) drive. There are several ways you can achieve this. For speed and simplicity, however, the first method – using the right mouse button – is recommended.

Using the right mouse button

1 Select the Folders view. In the window on the left, select the folder that contains the file you want to copy or move.

2 In the window on the right, select the file you want to copy or move.

Instead of a single file you can copy/move multiple files (just select as shown in the last topic), or copy/move a folder using the same technique.

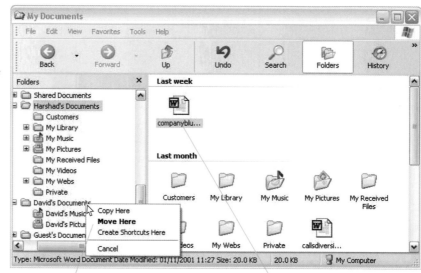

4 Click on the Move Here or Copy Here option.

3 Using the right mouse button drag the file you want to copy/move onto the destination folder or drive (in the window on the left) so that it is highlighted. Then release to display a shortcut menu.

Using the left mouse button

All of these operations can be carried out from My Computer or Windows Explorer.

In both cases, ensure Folders view is active: View menu, Explorer Bar, Folders (or simply click on Folders from the Standard Buttons toolbar).

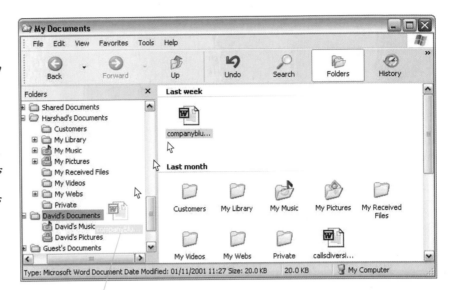

| Use the left mouse button to drag a file (or multiple files/folders) to the destination folder or drive in the window on the left.

2 To move/copy files to the same drive or to another drive, follow this simple technique:

You'll notice a little '+' symbol in a box if the file is going to be copied. Otherwise, the file will be moved.

Copy to another drive	Just drag
Move to another drive	Hold down the Shift key when dragging
Copy to same drive	Hold down the Ctrl key when dragging
Move to same drive	Just drag

Using Cut, Copy, Paste

Cut, Copy and Paste techniques shown here can also be used to select text or graphics in one program and move/copy them into another. A temporary Windows area, called the Clipboard, holds items cut or copied.

You can also use Cut, Copy and Paste from the Edit menu or the Standard Buttons toolbar.

You can use Move To or Copy To Standard Buttons instead.

1 Right-click on a file.

2 From the shortcut menu click on Cut (to move) or Copy. Cut doesn't initially remove the file – it turns it gray until you Paste it (step 5). If you change your mind, press ESC.

3 Open a window for the folder you want to copy/ move the file into.

4 Right-click the mouse button in a blank area of the window.

5 Click on Paste from the shortcut menu.

Explicitly to a writable CD drive/Floppy drive

 Make sure there is a floppy disk in your floppy disk drive if you're copying or moving files there.

 Keep the Shift key pressed when selecting the floppy disk to Move the file instead of Copying it.

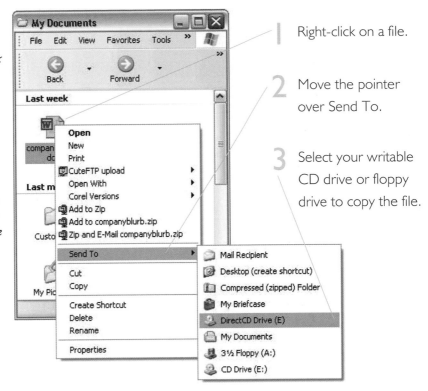

1 Right-click on a file.

2 Move the pointer over Send To.

3 Select your writable CD drive or floppy drive to copy the file.

 Click on the Close button (X) in the message balloon to ignore this message and to review the files later once you've built up the files you want written from other folders.

If you're writing files to a CD drive this message pops up in the notification area of the taskbar. Click on it to review the files temporarily waiting to be written to your CD – see page 157 for further details on how to write files to your writable CD drive.

Deleting Files/Folders

Deleting files and folders is easy and safe in Windows XP (see also the next topic, The Recycle Bin). Note that you can delete a file from wherever it is listed, although the My Computer display is shown here.

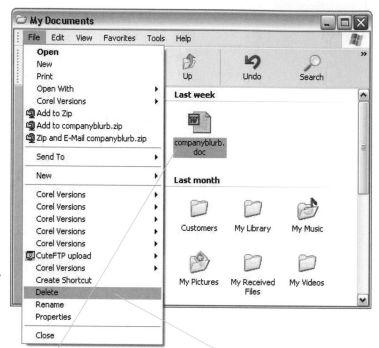

Press the Delete key on your keyboard, or click on the Delete button from the Standard Buttons toolbar instead.

Delete can also be chosen by right-clicking on the file and selecting it from the shortcut menu displayed.

1 Select one or more files/folders (see pages 52–53).

2 Click on Delete from the File menu.

You can also delete a file by dragging it onto the Recycle Bin icon on the desktop.

3 Click on Yes.

If you suddenly realise that you have made a mistake deleting one or more files, choose Undo Delete from the Edit menu or the Undo button from the toolbar straightaway. Alternatively, use the Recycle Bin to retrieve it (see next topic).

The Recycle Bin

Files that you delete from your floppy disk or from the Command Prompt don't go into the Recycle Bin.

The Recycle Bin is a place where deleted files are kept. They are not physically deleted from your hard disk until you 'empty' the Recycle Bin (or erase them within the Bin itself). The Recycle Bin therefore provides a safety net for files you may delete by mistake and allows you to easily retrieve them.

A drawback of the Recycle Bin is that from time to time, you'll have to empty it to free up disk space taken up by deleted files.

Restoring files

Recycle Bin

Double-click on the Recycle Bin icon from the desktop.

Ensure that you're using context sensitive task pane view – see page 49.

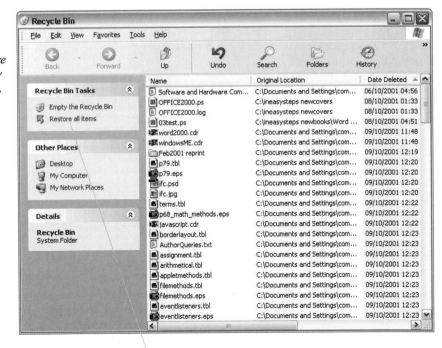

You can also restore whole folders containing other folders and/or files.

2   Click on **Restore all items**, or select a file/multiple files (as shown on pages 52–53) and this link changes to **Restore this item/ Restore the selected items** respectively.

Emptying the Recycle Bin

Recycle Bin

Double-click on the Recycle Bin icon from the desktop.

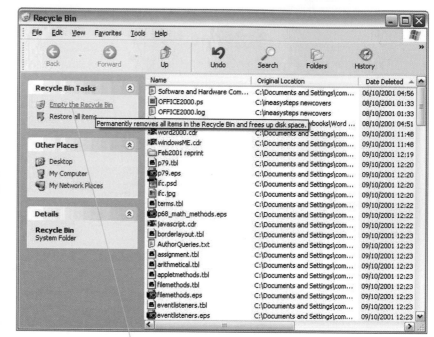

If you only want to erase certain files in the Bin, select them. Omit steps 2-3. Instead, click on Delete in the File menu. In the Confirm File Delete dialog, click on Yes.

2 Click on Empty the Recycle Bin task or select it from the File menu, to reclaim lost disk space.

3 Click on Yes.

Bypassing the Recycle Bin

If you want, you can have Windows XP *permanently* erase files or folders when you delete them – in other words, they aren't copied to the Recycle Bin.

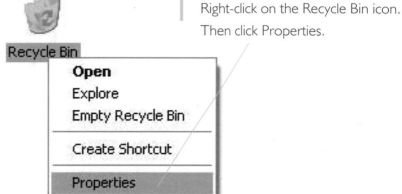

Right-click on the Recycle Bin icon. Then click Properties.

You can use a special technique which lets you specify that individual deletions bypass the Recycle Bin.

Don't follow steps 1–2. Instead, select the file/folder(s) you want to delete, then simply hold down one SHIFT key as you press the Delete key.

Finally, in the Confirm File Delete dialog, click on Yes.

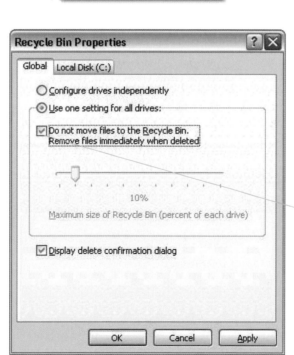

2 Click here to place a tick. Then click on OK.

Creating a New File/Folder

You can create new files in standard formats for use with specific programs installed on your computer. You can also create new folders within folders to further organise your work.

You can also create a new folder from the task pane.

You can also create a new file/folder on the desktop – just right-click in a blank area anywhere on the desktop.

Open a folder (from My Computer or Windows Explorer) you want to create a file or folder in and right-click on an empty part of the window.

2 Move the pointer over New, and then click on Folder to create a new folder. To create a file click on one of the file formats in the bottom section of the menu.

3 Type a name for the file/folder created and then press the ENTER key.

Renaming a File/Folder

You can rename a file/folder at any time. It is done very easily too, by simply editing the current name.

Use the same method to rename icons on the desktop. You won't be able to rename the Recycle Bin though!

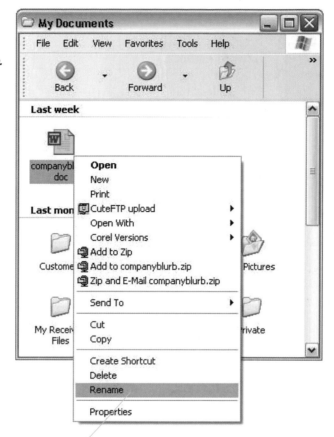

1 Right-click on a file/folder. Then click on Rename in the menu.

2 The current name will be boxed. Type a new name, or use the cursor arrow keys to position the cursor and only edit part of the name.

3 Press the ENTER key or click your mouse pointer outside the file name to confirm the new name.

Backtracking File Operations

Undo mistakes as soon as possible before performing too many other file operations.

If you accidentally delete, rename, copy or move a file, you can undo (reverse) the operation. Furthermore, you can even undo several preceding operations instead of just the last one (multi-level undo feature).

1 Click on the Edit menu from any folder. An Undo of the last file operation is displayed. Click on it and repeat if necessary.	or 2 Click on Undo from the Standard Buttons toolbar.

File Properties

Every file (and folder) has Properties. You can access the Properties dialog box for all in the same way. The purpose is twofold:

- to display basic information about the file
- to change settings for the file

There are some third party programs in this shortcut menu which you may not have.

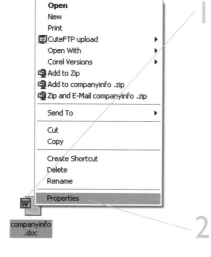

Right-click on a file to display the shortcut menu.

Click on Properties.

Click on the other tabs for further details.

Different Ways of Opening Files

There are several ways of opening files and their associated programs without first starting the programs.

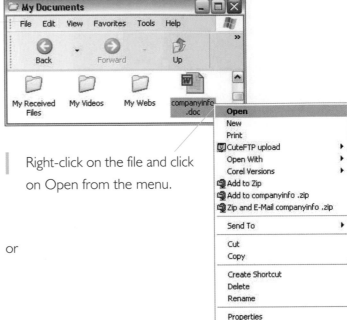

Opening files without first opening the programs works because different file formats are already associated with their programs.

To change an association or to create a new one select Tools, Folder Options, File Types tab from any folder window.

Right-click on the file and click on Open from the menu.

or

2 Click on the file to select it and then choose Open from the File menu.

or

3 Just double-click on the file icon.

or

Quite often you'll want to open a document you have been working on recently. Windows stores details of the latest 15 documents you've been using. Find them under the Start button, My Recent Documents for a faster access to them again.

Click on My Documents, My Pictures, or My Music for rapid access to these folders.

You can also access the My Documents folder from the Desktop provided 'Show My Documents on the Desktop' check box is ticked in the Tools menu (any folder window), Folder Options, View tab.

You can clear the documents that appear in My Recent Documents by right-clicking on the Start button, Properties, Start Menu tab, Customize button, Advanced tab, Clear List button.

4 Click on the required document from this list.

Searching for Files/Folders

You can also activate the Search Companion through the Start button, Search.

The Search feature in Windows XP is very fast and easy to use. The search can be based on partial file names, specific dates, types of files, size, and even text contained within the files. Once the desired files are found you can sort them in any order, change the view, open them, or perform other operations (including deleting, renaming, copying, displaying properties) – all from the search results displayed!

Click on the Search button from any folder window.

For specific types of files click on the appropriate link.

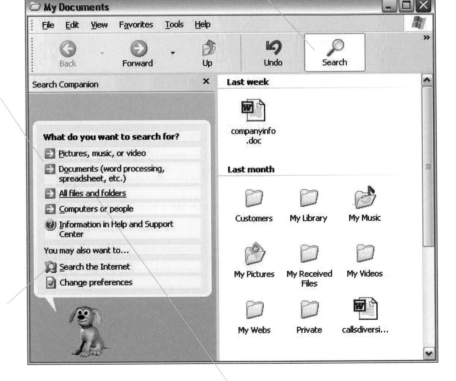

Click here to Search the Internet.

2 Click on All files and folders link in the Search Companion window.

3 Type in full/part name of the file or folder.

4 Type in possible text to search for within files.

5 To limit the search to specific drives or folders, select it from the drop-down list.

6 Click on the chevrons to specify other search criteria (see below).

7 Click here to start the Search.

 Click on the Back button to go back one step and refine or alter the choices you've made.

 If you did not find the files you were looking for, the Search Companion provides options to refine your search and try again.

 Once the Search has completed, the Search Results are displayed in the right window pane. You can perform file operations discussed in this chapter directly on the files listed.

Compressed Folders

This feature allows you to save disk space by compressing files/folders whilst still allowing them to be treated as normal folders by Windows. Compressed folders are distinguished from other folders by a zipper on the standard folder icon.

Compressed folders are compatible with other zip archive programs, like Winzip.

Creating a compressed folder

To create a compressed folder on the desktop, right-click on the desktop and then from the shortcut menu select New, Compressed (zipped) Folder.

From any folder window click on File, New, Compressed (zipped) Folder.

To create a compressed folder and copy a file into it at the same time: right-click a file, select Send To, Compressed (zipped) Folder.

The newly created compressed folder takes the same file name as the file copied (and therefore compressed) into it, but with a file extension of .zip.

2 A compressed folder with the default name of: New Compressed (zipped) Folder.zip is created. You can rename it right away by typing the new name, move it, or delete it as you would any other type of folder.

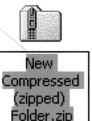

You can open a compressed folder in the same way as any other (by double-clicking on it).

Adding files/folders to a compressed folder

Simply drag any files or folders into a compressed folder and they will automatically be compressed there. By default, files will be copied to the compressed folder when you simply drag them there. If you wish to move them, press the Shift key at the same time. Note that this is a little different to how you copy/move files to normal folders.

Extracting files/folders from a compressed folder

Again, drag the files/folders selected out of the compressed folder and they'll be decompressed. A compressed version will still remain in the compressed folder, unless you press the Shift key at the same time, which will perform a move rather than a copy. To extract all files/folders from a compressed folder, right-click on it and then click on Extract All. The Extraction Wizard starts – follow the options here and specify the folder where you would like the contents extracted to.

Compressed Item Properties

Right-click on any file/folder in the compressed folder and choose Properties to see the compressed (or packed) size. Alternatively, you can compare the file sizes in the details view (View, Details).

Compressed Item Properties

Details
Name: companyinfo .doc
Type: Microsoft Word Document
Location: (Archive Root Directory)
Original Size: 20 KB
Date: 01/11/2001 11:27

Attributes
☐ Read-only   ☐ Hidden   ☐ System

ZIP Information
CRC32:   D620016E
Index: 0
Compression: Deflated
Packed Size: 3 KB

OK

Creating Scraps

A *scrap* is a piece of text copied/moved into a folder or onto the desktop, so that it can then be used over and over again in other documents by simply dragging it in place. This technique serves the same purpose as the Cut, Copy and Paste operations described on page 56, but it's more intuitive.

Drag the text with your left mouse button to create the scrap right away. Keep the Shift key pressed when dragging it to move the text block out instead of copying it.

1 Drag over text you want to create a *scrap* for.

2 Right-click and drag the block of text onto the desktop or into a folder. From the menu displayed select Create Scrap Here or Move Scrap Here. A Document Scrap icon is created there.

Drag the Document Scrap icon onto the Recycle Bin icon to delete it, when no longer required.

3 Drag the newly created Document Scrap into another document as required and its contents will be copied there.

Working with Programs

Most of the time you will be using your computer to run a program (also called an application). Find out how to start, organise and manage your programs effectively in Windows XP.

Covers

Chapter Five

Starting and Closing your Programs

The Start button enables you to quickly start any program installed in your computer. When you install new programs (page 84) their entries automatically appear under All Programs alphabetically:

If you're using a program frequently, drag its icon onto the Start button and it will always appear as a pinned item at the top of the Start menu.

Don't waste time looking for a program from the long All Programs menu, select it from your most recently used programs here.

A name with a forward-arrow is a program group rather than an actual program. Move the pointer over it to display a cascaded menu of programs that are under it.

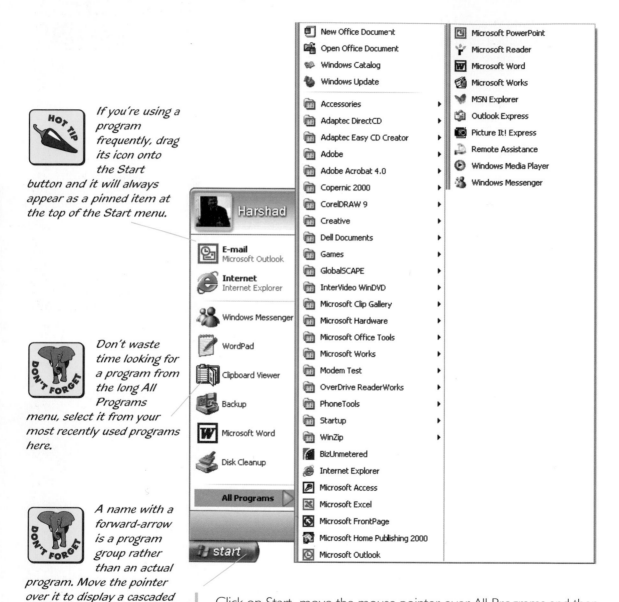

Click on Start, move the mouse pointer over All Programs and then click on a program name you want to start.

...cont'd

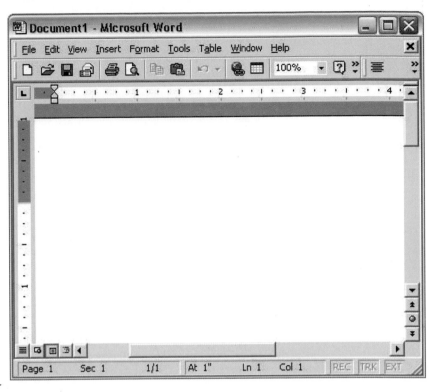

See page 80 for Windows XP's new taskbar grouping feature.

2   A button for the program/document appears on the taskbar and the program starts in its own window.

3   To quit from the program: click on the Close (X) button on the top right corner of the window, select Exit from the program's File menu, or right-click on the task button and choose Close.

Restore
Move
Size
Minimize
Maximize
Close   Alt+F4

Starting a Program using Run

Your DVD/CD-ROM drive may have a different letter assigned to it.

Windows XP has a special *Run* command which is usually used to run the setup program to install a new program, from say the A: floppy disk drive or the D: DVD/CD-ROM drive. However, you can use the Run command to start any program.

Click on the Run... option available from the Start button.

Click on the pull-down arrow to see previous commands used. Then click on one of these commands (if appropriate) instead of typing it in.

Browse... allows you to find the program and insert the path and name in the Open box.

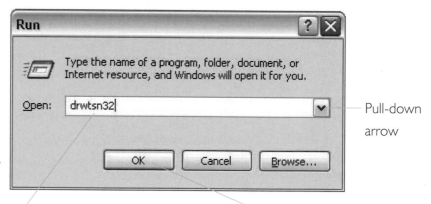

Pull-down arrow

2 Type in the full name of the program, including drive and path, if necessary.

3 Click on OK to start the program.

Creating a Shortcut

A *Shortcut* can provide easy access to a program you use frequently. You can place a shortcut on the desktop or in a folder.

Shortcuts can also be created to access other objects, including documents, folders, disk drives, printers, modems, faxes and even other computers.

Windows will not let you create shortcuts in certain pre-supplied folders e.g. My Computer, Printers and Control Panel.

1 Drag an item onto the desktop/folder using your right mouse button.

2 Release the mouse button once the item is in place to display a small menu.

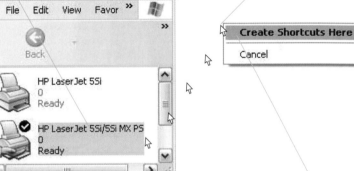

If you delete a shortcut, the file that it relates to is not automatically deleted and vice versa.

3 Click on the Create Shortcuts Here option. The shortcut will then appear. Note that the icon is different from the original – it has a small shortcut-arrow at the base.

You can also create a shortcut directly by simply dragging an item using the left mouse button.

HP LaserJet 5Si-5Si MX PS

Reorganising Start Menu Items

You can move program entries, folders and shortcuts to a new location within the Start menu.

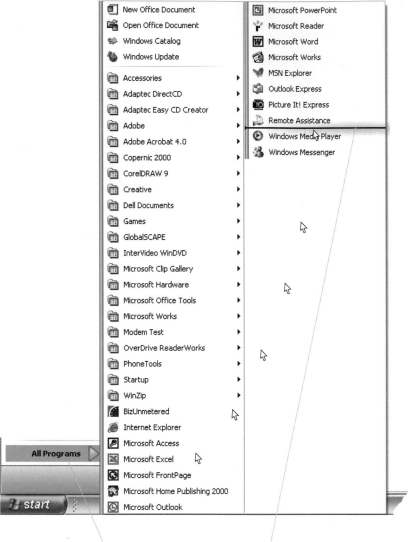

To move an item into the second-level menu, first drag it to the relevant program group entry (ones with forward arrows) to reveal it, then drag your item within it.

| | Click on the Start button and move the mouse pointer over All Programs.

2 | Move the mouse pointer over an item you want to move and simply drag it to the new location. A solid line indicates the insertion point.

Right-click on a Start menu item to reveal a short menu. From here you can pin the item to the top of the Start menu (see page 74) so that you don't spend too much time trying to find an important program. You can also delete and rename entries from this menu, and if you really mess it all up, just choose Sort by Name and all your Start menu entries will be sorted alphabetically.

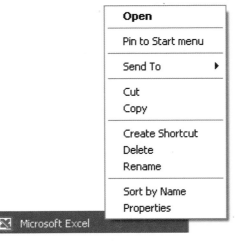

You can drag a program entry onto the Desktop (or another folder) to create a shortcut for that program there.

Changes you make to the Start menu entries do not affect the actual programs stored and installed on your system. These entries can be thought of as just shortcuts to start your programs quickly.

Adding Start menu items

As already mentioned, when you install new programs their entries are automatically created in the Start menu. However, to add back in any program entries removed or to add another type of entry like a frequently accessed folder, just follow these simple steps:

1 Create a shortcut for the item you want to add (see page 77).

2 Drag the shortcut onto the Start button, when the Start menu appears drag it to All Programs, and when that expands to all the entries, drag it to the appropriate place. Remember not to drop or let go of your shortcut until it has reached its final destination.

Taskbar Grouping

Windows creates a task button on the taskbar for every document you open within a program. Due to the *multitasking* capabilities of Windows, you can have several programs open at the same time, each with several open documents. This can result in a very cluttered taskbar, making it difficult to locate a particular task when you need to switch to it.

The new Windows XP feature, *taskbar grouping*, combines all the information for the same program into just one task button. It does this automatically once the number of task buttons builds up to a number that will not comfortably fit on the taskbar without considerable reduction in size.

Ensure Taskbar Grouping is active by right-clicking on the taskbar, clicking on Properties from the menu and placing a tick in the 'Group similar taskbar buttons' check box.

Grouped task button

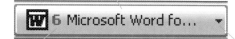

Number of documents grouped into this task button

Right-click on the task button to Cascade and Tile the document windows (as covered on page 31). Also, you can Minimize or Close all document windows, rather than each one individually.

Click here to display and select documents grouped

The pop-up menu displays the document name and the program that created it – click on any document to switch to it and bring its window to the forefront.

Task Manager

There's a new Task Manager program in Windows XP. As in the previous versions of Windows, you can use it to close a program that's stopped responding and to restart Windows if it has frozen, but now it also shows you what's going on in your computer.

1   Press Ctrl+Alt+Del keys to launch the Task Manager.

Windows XP is much more stable compared to earlier versions, so you shouldn't need to start the task manager as often.

2   Click on the Shut Down menu not only to select to restart Windows, but also to Stand By, Hibernate, Turn Off, Log Off and Switch User.

3   Click on the program that's not responding and then on the End Task button to close it.

Ending an operating system process could make Windows XP unstable.

4   Click on the Processes tab to see your programs as well as all the operating system processes. The Performance tab displays graphs for CPU and memory usage. If your PC is networked, the Networking tab shows the resources of your network connection. The Users tab shows the status of all users currently logged onto Windows XP.

Using Startup

The Startup feature allows a program or several programs to start automatically when you log on to Windows. Therefore, you can start work straightaway on a program that you always use.

1 Create a shortcut for a program you want to startup automatically (see page 77 and tip on page 79 for how to create a shortcut).

2 Drag the program shortcut into the Startup program group available from the Start menu, All Programs (see pages 78-79).

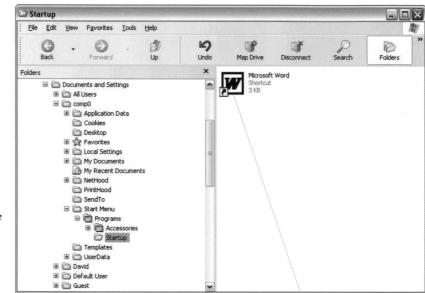

A shortcut to starting this Folders view in Windows Explorer is by right-clicking on the Start button and selecting Explore from the short menu.

or

2 Drag the program shortcut into the Startup folder. The path is: C:\Documents and Settings\Username\Start Menu\Programs\Startup (see pages 54-55 for help with moving items to folders)

3 The program(s) in the Startup folder (Microsoft Word in our example) will now start automatically each time you start Windows.

Starting Programs Minimised or Maximised

Sometimes you may want to start a program but not use it right away. You, therefore, need to set it up so that when it's started it is minimised automatically. When you are ready to use the program, you only need to click on its task button on the taskbar.

1 Create a shortcut for a program you want to start minimised (see page 77 and tip on page 79 for how to create a shortcut).

2 Right-click on the shortcut program icon and then select Properties from the menu.

This technique is quite useful if you're starting several programs automatically on Startup (see previous topic). You can then access them as you need to from the taskbar.

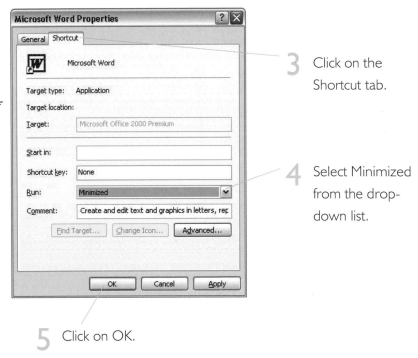

3 Click on the Shortcut tab.

4 Select Minimized from the drop-down list.

5 Click on OK.

To run programs maximised follow all the steps above, except select Maximized from the drop-down list in step 4. This is useful to set up if you always prefer to run certain programs in full window view.

Install and Uninstall Programs

You can add (install) new programs, add previously uninstalled components of an existing program, or remove them. You can also completely remove (or uninstall) a program you no longer require.

 Switch between Category and Classic views from the Control Panel task pane on the left.

1 Click on the Start button and then Control Panel (right pane).

2 Click on 'Add or Remove Programs' link (Category view) or double-click on its icon (Classic view).

 Sort the installed programs list (top right corner) by Size, Frequency of Use, or Date Last Used to help you pick the programs more easily.

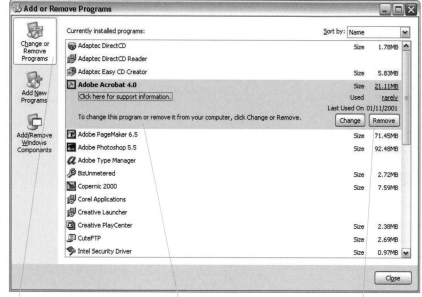

 Some programs have the Change and Remove functions combined into one button.

3 Make sure this button is selected.

4 Select a program from all the ones installed.

5 Click on Change/ Remove as appropriate.

 Some programs require you to insert the original program CD before you can continue.

6 Complete the further dialogs/messages which vary depending on the program selected. Most launch a tailor-made uninstall routine. Simply follow the on-screen instructions. If you remove a program including all of its components, Windows will ask for confirmation before it proceeds to deleting all the files.

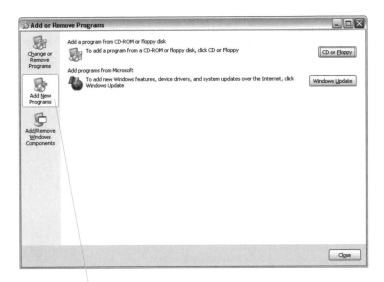

| Click here to install new programs.

You may need to restart Windows after a new program is added or removed.

2 The CD or Floppy button will start the Install Program wizard. Follow the instructions in this wizard to install your program.

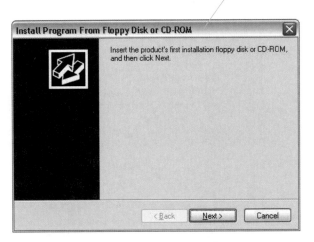

3 Windows Update (covered on page 168) will connect to the Internet and help you find and install programs from Microsoft, relating to Windows itself.

Alter Windows Components

Whether Windows XP was pre-installed when you bought your computer, or you upgraded/installed it yourself, you may want to alter the installed components at some stage.

1 Select 'Add or Remove Programs' from the Control Panel (follow steps 1–2 on page 84).

2 Click on Add/Remove Windows Components button to display this dialog box.

When you first open the Windows Components Wizard, if there's a tick against a component, then it's already installed.

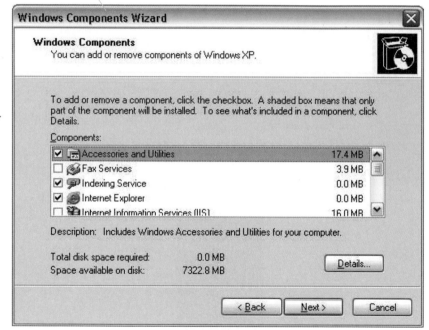

3 Click on a check box and place a tick to add that component. Also click to deselect a ticked box, which will remove that component. When you select a component, if the Details button is highlighted, you can click on it to select/deselect sub-components. A component with a shaded check box implies that you only want some of its sub-components to be installed. Click on Next to carry out the changes to your installation of Windows XP.

Program Compatibility

Most of your programs will run properly in Windows XP and so you'll probably never need to use this feature. However, you may have an older program or a game that was written specifically for an older version of Windows. If this is the case then:

1 Right-click on the old program icon or its shortcut in the Start menu (see page 79).

2 Select Properties from the menu displayed.

You can run the Program Compatibility Wizard available from the Help and Support Center instead, but the settings will not be saved once you close the program.

3 Click on the Compatibility tab.

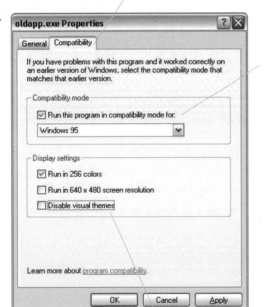

4 Check to run the program in compatibility mode and then select an older version of Windows from the drop-down list to run the program in.

5 Alter display settings if appropriate, depending on the requirements of your older program.

The Command Prompt

Windows XP does not rely on the older MS-DOS system. It has been rewritten to take out the MS-DOS dependency completely. However, for upward compatibility and to run some very old DOS programs, Windows XP includes an MS-DOS simulator in the form of the Command Prompt. To use it:

1   Click Start, point to All Programs, Accessories, and select Command Prompt.

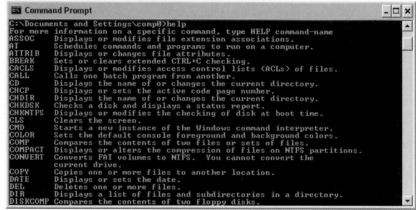

Press Alt+Enter to make the Command Prompt window full-screen if it's windowed, or vice versa.

2   Type MS-DOS commands at the > prompt. To display a list of commands and a brief description, issue the HELP command. For more detailed help on a specific command, type HELP followed by the command (or command/?). You can also type the name of your DOS program to run it.

3   When you have finished, click on the Close (X) button or type EXIT and press the Enter key.

The Internet and .NET Passport

Set up a new Internet connection, if you haven't already got one. Then, surf the net using the world's most popular web browser, Internet Explorer. The latest version is covered here exactly as it appears and works within Windows XP. Also build an Internet connection firewall to protect yourself online and learn about the new Microsoft .NET Passport service.

Covers

Chapter Six

New Internet Connection

Before you can use the Internet and browse the web, your computer needs to be set up to be connected to the Internet.

1 Click Start, Control Panel, Network and Internet Connections, Network Connections.

2 Select Create a new connection from the Network Tasks pane.

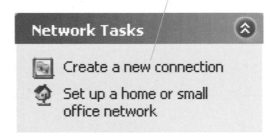

You can also get here via: Start, All Programs, Accessories, Communications, New Connection Wizard.

3 The New Connection Wizard launches. Click Next after each step.

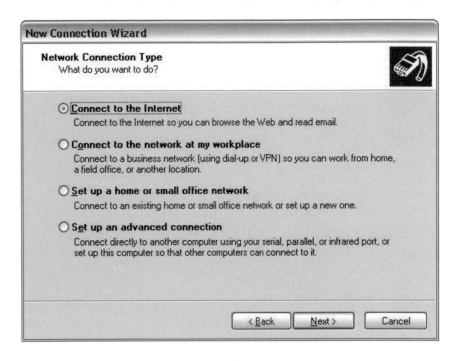

As an alternative you can run the connection software supplied by your Internet Service Provider (ISP).

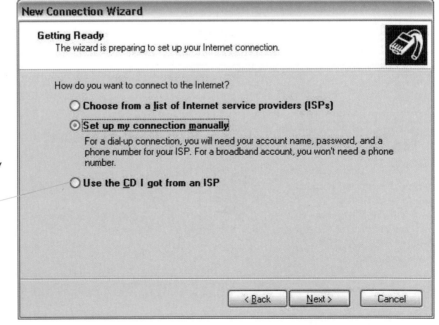

As part of this Wizard you'll be able to set up Internet Connection Sharing (ICS). This allows more than one person to connect to the Internet at any one time in a network environment.

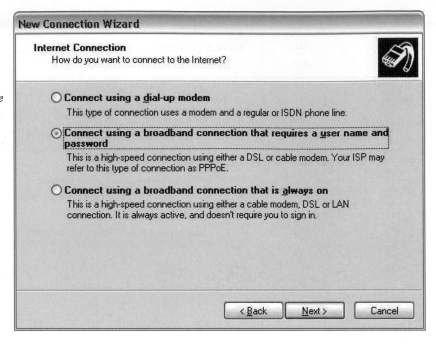

New Connection Wizard

Internet Connection
How do you want to connect to the Internet?

○ **Connect using a dial-up modem**
This type of connection uses a modem and a regular or ISDN phone line.

● **Connect using a broadband connection that requires a user name and password**
This is a high-speed connection using either a DSL or cable modem. Your ISP may refer to this type of connection as PPPoE.

○ **Connect using a broadband connection that is always on**
This is a high-speed connection using either a cable modem, DSL or LAN connection. It is always active, and doesn't require you to sign in.

`< Back` `Next >` `Cancel`

4   Decide on the type of connection to set up: dial-up or broadband. Select options as appropriate in other dialogs, which will vary depending on the choices you make. Click on the Back button if you make a mistake and want to select different options. Finally, click on the Finish button.

If your setup requires you to double-click a dial-up connection icon everytime you want to use the Internet, create a shortcut for it to your desktop (from the Wizard here or see page 77) for quick easy access.

LAN or High-Speed Internet

Local Area Connection
Enabled
3Com 3C905B-COMBO Fast Et...

5   Your Internet connection icon will be set up in the Network Connections folder.

Starting Internet Explorer

You don't have to start Internet Explorer to use the Internet.
You can surf the net from any folder window – see pages 44-47.

Internet Explorer

1 Double-click on the Internet Explorer icon from the desktop, choose it from Start menu, or from the Quick Launch toolbar.

2 You may need to click on the Connect button as mentioned on the previous page, otherwise Internet Explorer will start and connect you automatically, displaying the default Home page.

Select Tools, Internet Options to change the default Home page and to customise other settings (also available from Control Panel and IE icon Properties on the desktop).

A link can be a graphic or text. Text links are usually underlined and in a different colour.

3 Browse other web pages by clicking on (hyper)links – your mouse pointer changes to a hand when rested over a link.

Browsing the Web

Every page on the web has a unique address, called a URL (Uniform Resource Locator) or simply a web address. You see these advertised everywhere – newspapers, magazines and on television. To display a web page:

If you just type 'ineasysteps' and press Ctrl+Enter, the rest of the address is added for you.

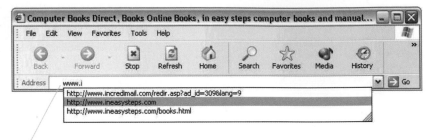

| Click in the Address bar and type the URL of the website you want to visit. Then press the Enter key or click on Go arrow.

Internet Explorer assumes that your web page starts with http:// at the beginning so you don't have to type this part in. So, for example, to visit Microsoft's home page, just enter:

www.microsoft.com

AutoComplete

When you type in an address, Internet Explorer tries to finish it based on sites you've visited before. In this way, typing:

www.i

The Address bar is on by default in Internet Explorer.
Further details on it are on page 45.

(for example) as above is likely to suggest addresses you may want to visit in a drop-down list – click on one that may apply. If the drop-down list is quite big you can ignore it and continue typing a bit more of the address to automatically shrink the drop-down list. This may make the selection a little easier.

You can click on the down-arrow next to the address box at any time for a list of addresses you've entered recently.

To turn off AutoComplete, click on Tools menu, Internet Options, Content tab, AutoComplete button.

Browser buttons

Some of the buttons on the Standard Buttons toolbar change automatically when you access the Internet (see page 44). This is to help you navigate and browse the web more easily rather than browse local files and folders on your computer. The most useful buttons when browsing the web are:

Activate the Links toolbar (see page 46) to view your major websites.

Back — Return to the page you just left. Click on the little down-arrow to the right to display a list from which you can select to go back several pages.

Forward — Once you've gone back a few pages you may want to go forward again. To go forward several pages click on the arrow to the right.

Stop — Click this button to abort downloading of a slow page so you can look at something else.

Refresh — Click this button to reload the page to ensure that you're seeing the very latest version.

Home — If you really get lost click this button and it will return you to the default Home page set up when you start Internet Explorer.

The last three of these buttons (Stop, Refresh, Home) replace Standard buttons when you access the Internet.

Other useful buttons that appear when browsing the web are Search, Favorites, Media and History. They are covered in the topics that follow in this chapter.

These buttons are not exclusive to the Internet – they are also used when browsing local information in your computer.

Searching the Internet

Search can also be started by clicking on the Start button, Search, Search the Internet.

1 Click on the Search button from the Standard Buttons toolbar or select it from View, Explorer bar.

Select Tools, Show Related Links to list sites that have something in common and further info on the current website displayed.

2 Select an option, type a word/phrase and click on Search.

3 Click on any link in the Search bar to load its page in the right pane.

Using a different Search Engine

If you don't find what you're looking for try another search engine. Click on the Next button or the little arrow to select another one from a menu. Your keywords will be sent there automatically.

Click on New to start a fresh Search.

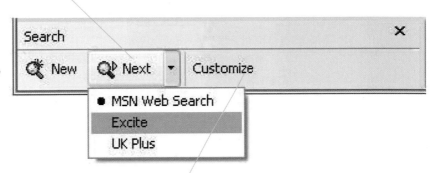

Customising the Search

Click on the Customize button to alter the search engines that are used to carry-out your searches.

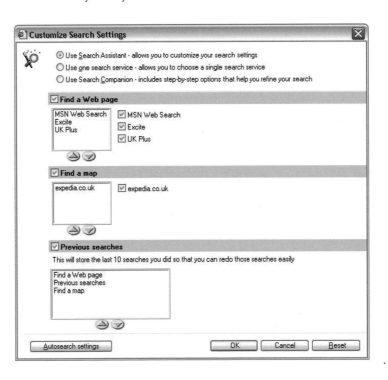

Bookmark Favourites

Favourites are sites you have previously visited and deemed worthy of revisiting. Note the American spelling (Favorites) within the product rather than British English (Favourites).

Click on the Favorites button from the Standard Buttons toolbar or select it from View, Explorer bar.

Click on your favourite links here (from the Favorites bar) to display their websites in the right pane.

Creating your own Favourites

Some websites will invite you to click on a link to add their page to your favourites listing automatically. For example, visit www.ineasysteps.com and click on:

When you are surfing the Internet and you find a web page you think you'll want to revisit, then instead of remembering its web address, click on the Add... button at top of the Favorites bar. This will create a link of the currently displayed page to your list of favourites. You can also easily create your own folders here to put your favourite links into and make the content available offline.

Organising your Favourites

Click on the Organize... button at top of the Favorites bar to rename, delete and manage into folders all your favourite links. You can also drag them around to change their display order.

Media Bar Playback

The Media bar is a tool designed to play music and video clips, not only from your own computer but also from abundance of media content available on the Internet. In fact, when you're online and you activate the Media bar, the WindowsMedia.com site opens offering you to a choice of media to play, including radio stations, movie clips and trailers, concerts, etc...

1 Click on the Media button from the Standard Buttons toolbar or select it from View, Explorer bar.

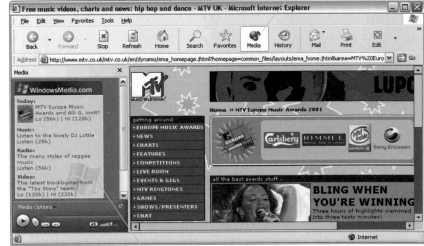

Many clips you play will automatically transfer the file to Windows Media Player and play it there. Media Player is covered in Chapter 11.

2 Click on today's links to play them or select other media from the Media Options drop-down list.

3 Use Play/Pause, Stop, Previous track, Next track, Mute and Volume slider to control the playback. To play the clip in a separate window click the Undock player button. To transfer playback to the main Media bar click on the Redock player button.

Undock player button

Redock player button

History Bar

1 Click on the History button from the Standard Buttons toolbar or select it from View, Explorer bar.

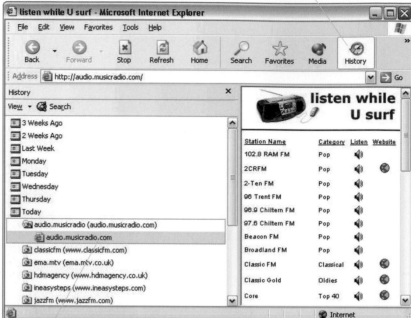

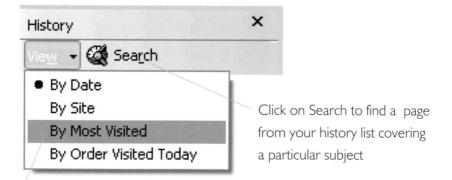

You can change how long the history is kept. Go to Tools, Internet Options. From the General tab alter the 'Days to keep pages in history'.

From here you can also click on the Clear History button to wipe off all the current history pages.

2 Click on a day or a previous week (in history) and then on a web page to redisplay it in the right pane.

Click on Search to find a page from your history list covering a particular subject

If you can't find the page you want try sorting the history list in a different way by clicking on View

Printing Web Pages

Quite often, you'll come across material on the web that will be useful as reference in hard copy. You can therefore print the current web page by one of these methods:

1. Click on the Print button in the Standard Buttons toolbar

2. Select Print from the File menu and then make further selections in the Print dialog box

3. Press Ctrl+P

4. Since web pages are designed for the monitor, they don't always print as expected, so select Print Preview from the File menu first, and then when satisfied click on the Print button (to avoid wasting paper).

If you only want to print a few paragraphs of text from a web page, highlight them using your mouse and then in the Print dialog box, click on the Selection option.

Choose the Options tab in the Print dialog box to select to 'Print table of links' and 'Print all linked documents' from the current web page.

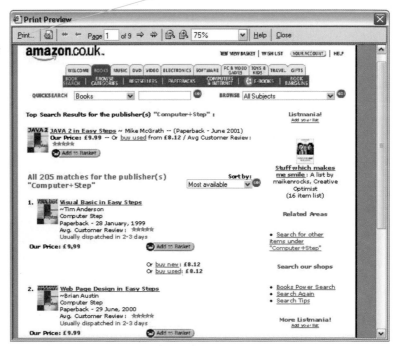

The Print Preview window has controls to navigate through pages and to zoom in/out. To change the margins, header/footer, page orientation, click on the Setup button.

Image Toolbar and Resizing

Many web pages will contain images. A new feature in Internet Explorer will display a small image toolbar if you hold your mouse pointer over an image without clicking on it. This toolbar consists of four buttons:

The image toolbar will not appear on very small images.

1 Saves the image.

2 Prints the image.

3 Attaches the image to an email message so you can send it to someone.

4 Opens My Pictures folder so you can keep a copy of the image there by dragging it across.

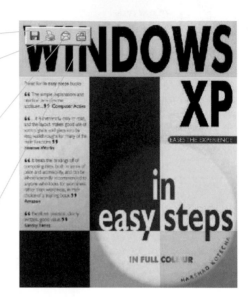

If you don't find the Image toolbar and the Resize button useful, click on Tools, Internet Options, Advanced tab, scroll down to the Multimedia section and uncheck 'Enable Image Toolbar' and 'Enable Automatic Image Resizing' respectively.

The Image toolbar can also be turned off by right-clicking on it and selecting 'Disable Image Toolbar'.

If you view the image on its own rather than as part of a web page, a resize button may appear at the bottom right corner. This implies that Internet Explorer has automatically resized the image to make it fit into the window.

1 Click to enlarge the image to its normal size.

2 Click again to resize the image to fit into the window.

Internet Connection Firewall

Windows XP can set up a firewall to guard against outsiders gaining access to files on your computer whilst you're online. To set up an Internet Connection Firewall (ICF):

ICF can also be set up as part of the New Internet Connection Wizard discussed at the start of this chapter.

I   Click on Start, Control Panel, Network and Internet Connections, Network Connections.

2   Right-click on your Internet connection icon and then select Properties from the menu.

3   Click on the Advanced tab.

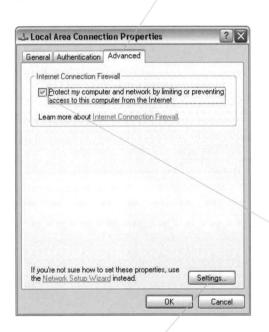

4   Click in this box to put a tick mark.

5   Click on the Settings button to select services you use. Many of the options here are advanced – you may want to check with your Internet Service Provider. If you're not sure, leave them unchecked initially for maximum protection.

.NET Passport

Microsoft has come up with a new concept called .NET Passport. This simplifies the way you access many of the websites and services on the Internet. Instead of filling out online forms and remembering different passwords each time, Passport-enabled sites will let you straight in using your email address.

To create a .NET Passport

Passport may give Microsoft too much power. They can compile an information database from all the Passport-enabled sites you visit.

1 Click on the Start button, Control Panel, User Accounts and then select your account.

2 Click **Set up my account to use a .NET Passport** option.

Information in your Passport is protected by encryption and you're always in control of deciding who has access to it.

3 The .NET Passport Wizard will start. Click on the Next button to continue. A Wizard is a series of dialog boxes providing information and allowing you to make choices from options presented so that any task can be completed easily. There are specific Wizards throughout Windows XP for other tasks.

You'll see a dialog box from time-to-time asking you to wait while the wizard downloads information from the Internet.

.NET Passport Wizard

Do you have an e-mail address?

With a Microsoft® .NET Passport, you can use your e-mail address and a single password to sign in to all participating Web sites and services.

Do you have an e-mail address?

⊙ Yes.

○ No, I would like to open a free MSN.com e-mail account now.

Don't want free MSN.com e-mail? Just open an e-mail account with another provider and then return to this wizard to register it as your .NET Passport.

< Back   Next >   Cancel

Click on the Back button to change options from the previous box, or Cancel to abandon the procedure altogether. Otherwise, continue completing the dialogs and selecting Next until the Finish button appears.

.NET Passport Wizard

What is your e-mail address?

Please type your e-mail address. If you already have a .NET Passport, or if you have an MSN® Hotmail® or MSN.com e-mail address, type that address here. (Hotmail and MSN.com e-mail addresses are already .NET Passports.)

E-mail Address

yourname@company.com

< Back   Next >   Cancel

4   Select your options as shown and click Next at each stage.

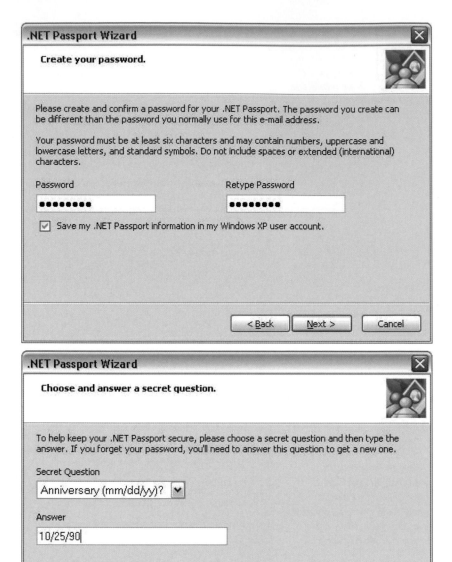

5 Create your password and a secret question plus answer.

6   The next box will ask you where you live. If you forget your password, you'll need to provide this information as well as answer your secret question to get a new password. Click Next to continue.

7   Then the .NET Passport terms of use will be displayed in a little scrollable window. This forms an agreement between yourself and Microsoft. You'll be able to print this out and only proceed after you select the option "I accept the agreement".

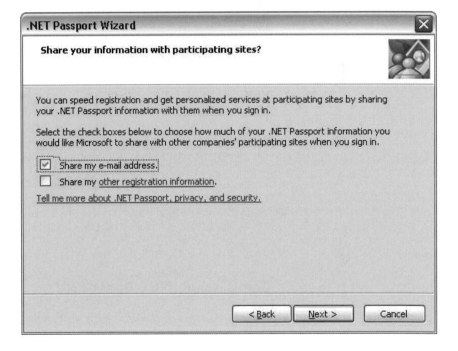

8   Here you decide how much of your personal information you share with other (implying other than Microsoft) participating sites when you sign in using your Passport. "Other registration information" includes your geographic location.

9 Finally, your .NET Passport is set up. Click on the Finish button.

10 You'll automatically receive an email asking you to verify your email address. Click on the link in this email to verify your email online.

Using your .NET Passport

Your Passport data travels with you as you visit different sites. To Sign In at a Passport-enabled site click on this button:

Some sites will allow you to type in your email and password directly in the Passport sign-in box without first having to click on the sign-in button.

You'll then be able to type in your email address and password in the sign-in box that appears.

Once you sign in to one Passport-enabled site, you can sign in to any others by just clicking on their Sign In button. You will not have to provide your email and password each time.

To Sign Out simply click on this button:

Clicking on this button from one site will sign you out of all other Passport-enabled sites you've been using.

To create your Passport wallet

You'll need to create a Passport wallet if you want to use the **Passport express purchase** service. A passport wallet is a convenient way to store your credit card and billing/delivery address details online so that you don't need to keep retyping them everytime you want to buy something online. To create your Passport wallet visit the secure site:

https://wallet.passport.com

Microsoft® Passport

Wallet Service

🔒 Secure Site   **Enter payment information**   Sign Out .net   .net Passport

1) Payment information

Microsoft Passport wallet accepts these payment types

VISA

Card type:	Visa ▼
Card number:	
Name on card:	
Expiration:	10 ▼ / 2003 ▼
Description:	Visa

Type a description that will help you identify this payment type.

The information you provide is saved securely in your wallet at Microsoft so you won't have to retype it every time you make a purchase at participating sites.

You can use your wallet from any computer connected to the Internet.

2) Billing address

First name:		Postal code:	
Last name:		Country/region:	United Kingdom ▼
Address line 1:		Phone:	
Address line 2:		E-mail:	
City:		Description:	
State/province:			

Type a description that will help you identify this address.

3) [Save] [Cancel]

Using Passport express purchase

Once you've created your Passport wallet you can use the information stored in it to make online purchases easily and securely at any participating site by clicking on this link:

Passport member services

To amend your .NET Passport or wallet details, or if you forget your password, or if you need help, visit:

http://www.passport.com/memberservices.asp

To see a list of .NET Passport sites visit: http://www. passport.com/ directory.asp

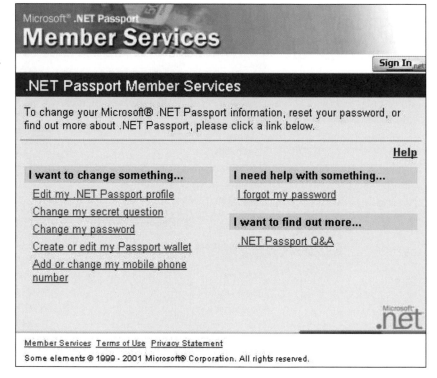

Windows Messenger and Email

A growing number of people are using *instant messaging*. This is the ability to communicate (instantly) with other online users. Windows Messenger is Microsoft's version of the instant messaging software. It is part of the new .NET services Microsoft is developing and you will need to set up a .NET passport (as covered in the previous chapter) before you can use Windows Messenger. Also covered here is Outlook Express – the email program included with Windows XP – and how it integrates with Windows Messenger.

Covers

Chapter Seven

See Who is Online

Open Windows Messenger from the notification area in your taskbar by double-clicking on the little "people" icon or select it from the Start menu, All Programs, Windows Messenger.

Then click on the sign-in link and sign in using your .NET Passport. Once online you can see who else is online, provided they have been added to your Contacts list (see below), and have a conversation with them over the Internet.

 You can call yourself whatever you want online – select Tools, Options... and type a name in My Display Name box.

 Click on My Status arrow to appear Busy, On The Phone, Out To Lunch, etc... to your online contacts.

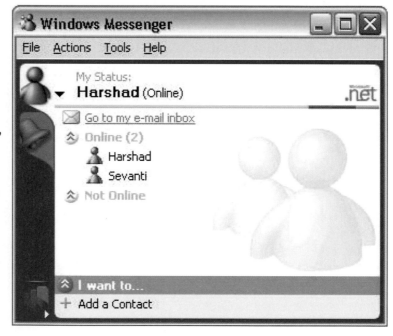

 Messenger offers to send your contacts emails explaining how they can get a Passport account so they can communicate with you online.

Adding a Contact

Click on Tools, Add a Contact... or select it from the Actions pane at the bottom. Then add a contact by entering their email address, asking Messenger to search Hotmail's directory or your own email address book. Your contacts will need a Passport account if they're to be found.

Sending an Instant Message

Double-click on a name from your online list (see previous page) to open a window so that you can have a conversation with that person.

If your contact is not online, still double-click on the name to open your email program with your contact's email address entered. Now you can quickly send an email, perhaps to arrange a convenient time for a chat.

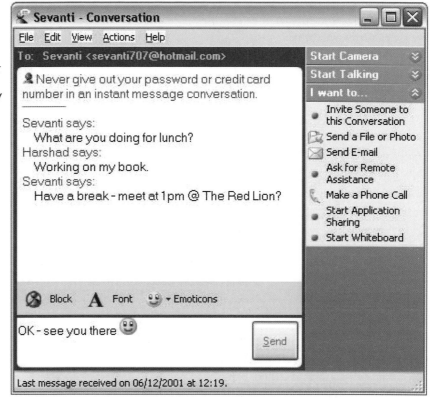

You don't have to wait for a response before you send another message.

Type your messages (one at a time) in the bottom part of the window and then press the Enter key or click on the Send button. You'll see your messages and the responses from your contact in the larger area above.

It's possible to keep multiple conversations going – each in a separate window. Simply select another online contact from the original Messenger window.

The Block icon stops a contact from sending you messages and seeing you online, Font allows you to change the text font and colour and Emoticons can be inserted in your messages, representing expresssions like happy face, sad face, a wink.

From the right pane you can invite someone else into the conversation and establish a video and/or voice link, provided you have the necessary hardware.

Setting Up Outlook Express

Outlook Express is a cut-down version of Microsoft Outlook, which is part of Microsoft Office.

Outlook Express is a program that may be used to manage your emails. The latest version (v6) is inluded with Windows XP. Start it from the desktop shortcut icon, the quick launch area on the taskbar, or the start menu.

Outlook Express

The first time you start Outlook Express, a wizard will prompt you to set up your email account. Most Internet Service Providers (ISPs) now set up your account automatically within Outlook Express. However, if you need to do it manually or create additional email addresses click on the Tools menu, Accounts, Mail tab. Then click on the Add button and select Mail to start the Internet Connection Wizard:

Customise Outlook Express via Tools, Options...

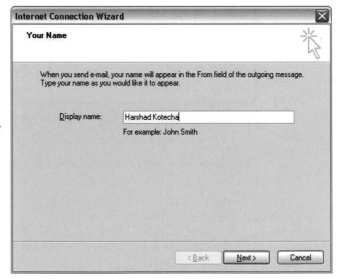

Follow the instructions in this wizard. You will need your Internet email address, the server names for incoming and outgoing mail, etc. Your ISP will provide you with all the settings that you will need to enter here.

Checking your Mail

Mail which is sent to you is stored by your service provider, and downloaded to you when you request it and connect online.

| Start Outlook Express and then click on Send/Recv.

Click on the arrow next to the Send/Recv button and select Receive All if you don't have anything to send.

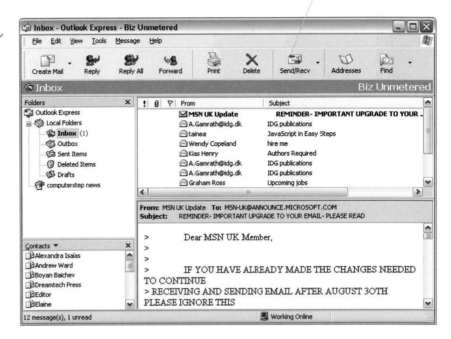

2 If you're on a dial-up connection, a Dial-up Connection box will appear. Confirm connection to your service provider, after checking your User name and Password.

3 Any mail that you have received will appear in the Inbox folder and display as one-line messages in the upper right window pane.

To delete a message, drag the message to the Deleted Items folder in the left pane.

The other four folders are used as follows: outgoing mail waiting to be sent is stored in the Outbox (and normally sent in the same connection session as incoming mail is delivered); the mail is then transferred into the Sent Items folder; any mail that is not required may be moved to the Deleted Items folder, and unfinished mail not yet ready to send is stored in the Drafts folder.

Reading Messages

As mentioned in the previous topic, downloaded messages are stored in your Inbox. To read them, first ensure that the Inbox folder is selected. All your messages in the upper right pane use the following standard:

 A message line prefixed with a closed yellow envelope and the entry in bold type is an Unread message.

A message line prefixed with an open white envelope and the entry in light type is a Read message.

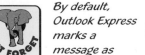

By default, Outlook Express marks a message as 'read' when it has been previewed for 5 seconds.

Click on a message line to preview it in the lower pane. To open the message in its own special editor window double-click on the message:

displays previous message   displays next message

To print your message on the default printer, click on the Print button, or choose Print... from the File menu for the Print dialog box.

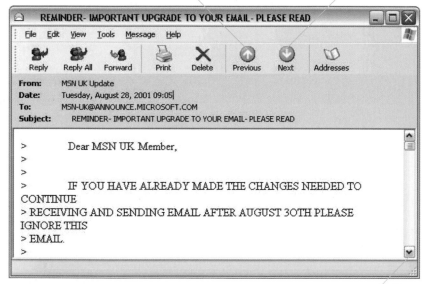

scroll through your message and click on the Close window button when you have finished

Replying to a Message

Step 2 – to send the reply to all the recipients of the message you were reading, click on the Reply All button instead:

To forward a message, follow step 1. Click on the Forward button:

Carry out steps 3-4.

Choose other buttons, as appropriate, before sending your message. For example, Spelling to check your text for errors, Priority to tag the message as high or low priority for your recipient.

Open a message in the preview window or the special editor, as discussed in the previous topic.

2 Click on the Reply button in the toolbar.

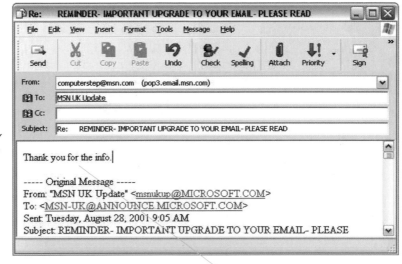

3 Type your reply here.

4 Click on Send button (or File, Send Message). If you have several messages, batch them up by choosing File, Send Later. Then press the Send/Recv button to send them all together.

Sending File Attachments with your Email

Before step 4 above, click on this button. Then select a file from the Insert Attachment dialog box and click on another Attach button there to insert it with your email.

Composing a New Message

Click on the arrow to the right of this button and then Select stationery... to choose a design for your email. You can even create a new design to personalise your message style from here.

Click on the Create Mail button (available from any Outlook Express folder except the editor).

You can also open the New Message window by double-clicking on any of your Contacts (page 115) – their email address will automatically be entered in the To: box.

This message uses the 'Party Invitation' stationery

2 Type the name of the recipient in the To: box and click on the Check button to check the name or click on the To: button to launch the Address book:

To manage your Address Book click on this button:

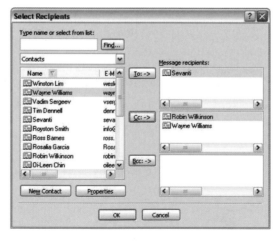

3 Select names and click on the To & Cc (courtesy copy) buttons to add as many names as you want.

4 Click OK and follow steps 3–4 on page 117.

Messenger from Outlook Express

Microsoft have designed Windows Messenger and Outlook Express to work well together.

Just as you can automatically start a New Message email window by selecting a Messenger contact not online, when you are in Outlook Express and online, all your Messenger contacts will appear in your contacts folder:

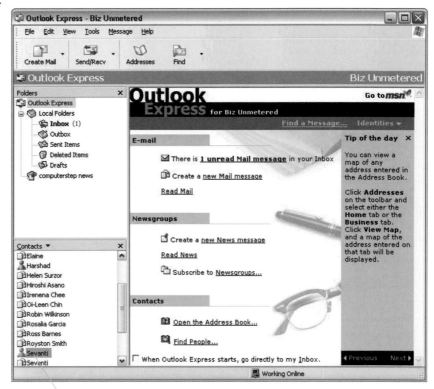

Double-click on a Windows Messenger contact online. You will easily recognise them because they will be prefixed by the Messenger icon.

2 A Messenger conversation window will open (see page 113). Here you can send and receive messages interactively in an online session. If you and your contact have a microphone and headset, you can switch the conversation from text to voice through the Start Talking task pane.

Sending Web Pages as Email

It is possible and very easy to send a complete web page as an email.

As an alternative, when you're browsing the Web using Internet Explorer, click on the Mail toolbar button and select Send Page... to send the current page being viewed to someone.

| From the Create Mail drop-down list in Outlook Express, select Web Page...

If the web page you're sending is complicated your recipient will receive it as a read-only or attached file.

2 Type in the URL of the web page you want to send or an address of any page formatted using HTML code.

Type a URL in your email text and it will automatically be converted to a hyperlink that your recipient can click on to visit that web site.

3 The web page is inserted in your email to send (see page 118).

Printing and Fonts

To produce hard copies of the documents you've created in an application, information from the web, or your email messages, you will need a printing capability.

This chapter covers everything you need to know to understand and manage printing and fonts.

Covers

Chapter Eight

Printer Setup

Before you set up your printer to work with Windows XP, ensure that it is connected to your computer. If it is a plug-and-play printer connected via a USB port, then Windows XP will install it for you automatically – you can therefore skip this topic.

Click on the Start button, Printers and Faxes.

If you have not yet set up any printers, only the Add Printer icon is visible in the Printers and Faxes window.

2 Click on the Add a printer link in the Printer Tasks pane.

If you have more than one printer installed, change the default printer if necessary – right-click on its icon and select Set as Default Printer. This then becomes the printer your applications use automatically.

A Network printer can be set up instead of a local one through the Add Printer Wizard.

3 The Add Printer Wizard starts. Follow the instructions to add an icon for your new printer in the Printers and Faxes window.

Fonts

All the fonts installed on your computer are usually stored in one place: Fonts folder under the Control Panel. To view them:

1 Click on the Start button, Control Panel, Switch to Classic View and then double-click on the Fonts folder icon.

Fonts

If you prefer to only work with Microsoft's TrueType fonts, select Tools, Folder Options, TrueType Fonts tab, and then check the box 'Show only TrueType fonts in the programs on my computer'.

2 Double-click on the font you want to preview.

3 To add new fonts select File, Install New Font...

4 To delete a font right-click on it and select Delete.

5 Use the View menu for further information about fonts. For example, click on the List Fonts By Similarity option and then use the drop-down box here to select the base font. Windows XP will now list all fonts and tell you if they're Very similar, Fairly similar or Not similar to the base font selected.

Printing Documents

Once your printer is set up in Windows XP, printing is easy. You can print a document from the program that created it or by dragging the file onto the printer icon.

From the menu

Click on the print button

in the toolbar to quickly print one copy of the whole document to the default printer, and thus avoid the Print dialog box altogether.

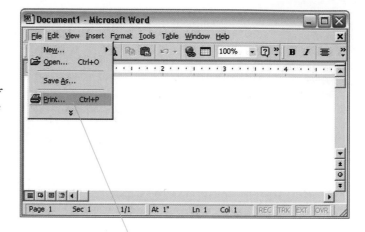

Click on File, Print... from your application (after typing some text or opening a document you want to print).

Select Print Preview from the File menu first to ensure your document will print as you expect.

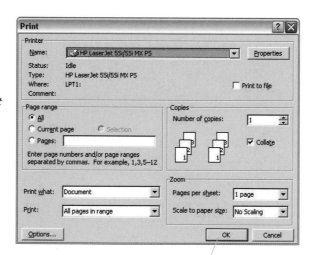

2 From the Print dialog box, amend any options, as required (e.g. Pages to print, Number of copies), then click on OK.

Using drag-and-drop

 Avoid having too many printers. When you buy a new printer, delete the setup for the old one if it's no longer going to be used – right-click on its icon and select Delete.

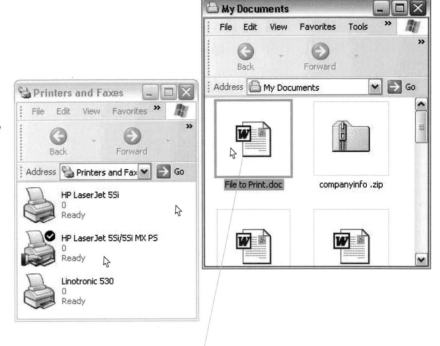

Drag out a file you want to print.

2 Place the file icon on the printer you want to use to print the file.

You can have a shortcut icon for a specific printer rather than the actual printer icon – if you are going to use the drag-and-drop technique often, create a shortcut icon for your main printer on the desktop (see page 77).

Once you've dragged-and-dropped a file onto the printer icon, the program associated with the file is started and so is the printing – automatically!

Print Management

When you submit a document for printing, Windows first spools it to a temporary disk file rather than sending it directly to the printer. You can send several files for printing at once. They will queue up (get spooled) in succession for your selected printer. This allows you to intercept and control their output from the print queue before they are physically printed.

You can also open the print queue by double-clicking on the small printer icon in the notification area (usually in the bottom right corner) after a print job is submitted.

HP LaserJet 5Si/5Si MX PS

1 Double-click on the printer icon your jobs are submitted to.

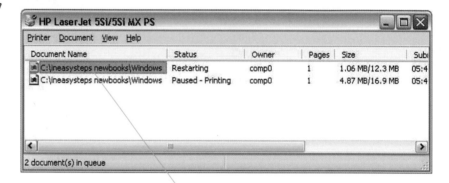

Click on Pause Printing from the Printer menu to make the printer pause e.g. to change the paper type.

Also from the Printer menu, select Cancel All Documents to delete all documents from the print queue to abandon their printing. The current job may finish printing if its pages have already been sent to the printer's memory.

2 Right-click on the Document Name you want to change the status of. From the short menu select:

Pause   – to halt printing of a document
Resume   – to continue printing of a paused document
Restart   – to start printing the document from the beginning
Cancel   – to remove the document from the print queue
Properties   – to change the print priority by dragging a slider

You can change the status of several documents at once if you have multiple selections: hold down the Ctrl key and click on each document in turn, right-click on one and choose an option to apply to all selected documents.

Configuration

You can configure many of your printer settings depending on the type of printer you have.

1   From the Printers and Faxes folder, right-click on the printer icon you want to configure.

2   In the shortcut menu, click on Properties.

 Click on the Print Test Page button (from the General tab) after you have first installed your printer to ensure that it works as expected. If it doesn't, Windows Printing Troubleshooter will guide you through correcting the problem.

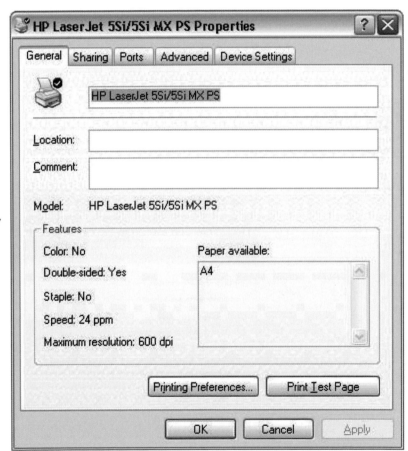

3   Click on the appropriate tab and change the settings, as required. Finally, click on OK.

Troubleshooting

Printing problems are common. If you experience difficulties, use Windows XP's Printing Troubleshooter to resolve them.

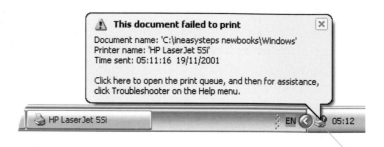

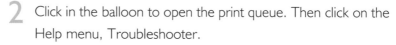

1 Whenever there is a problem (e.g. paper jam), the printer icon in the notification area displays a red warning circle with a question mark and a warning balloon pops up.

You can also start the Printing Troubleshooter from the main Help and Support Center via the Start button.

2 Click in the balloon to open the print queue. Then click on the Help menu, Troubleshooter.

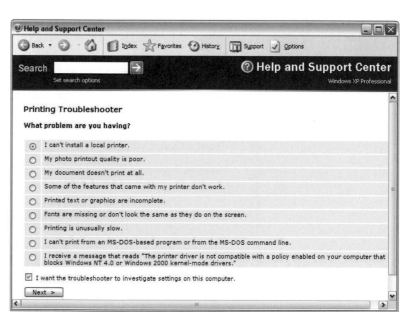

3 Follow the instructions in the Printing Troubleshooter Wizard.

Networking

A Network is a group of computers linked together. There is a built-in networking capability within Windows XP allowing you to share files, printers and an Internet connection between two or more computers in your home or at the workplace.

Before you start to set up networking, ensure that your computers have Network Adapters (also known as Network Interface Cards – NIC) installed. These control the communication of one computer with another in the network. All computers also need to be physically connected, via the network adpters, using special cables and connectors.

Covers

Chapter Nine

Network Setup Wizard

Ensure that the computers in your network are physically connected with network adapters and cables before running the Network Setup Wizard. Also, run this wizard on the computer that will share its Internet connection with the other computers first.

| Click Start, Control Panel, Network and Internet Connections, Network Connections.

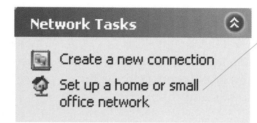

2 Select 'Set up a home or small office network' link from the Network Tasks pane.

Click Next on all the Wizard dialogs that follow after making your choices. Finally click on Finish.

3 Click Next to begin setting up your network.

The Network Setup Wizard also sets up Internet Connection Sharing (ICS). This allows all PCs in a network to browse the web and use email simultaneously, with just one PC needing an Internet connection (provided it's turned on).

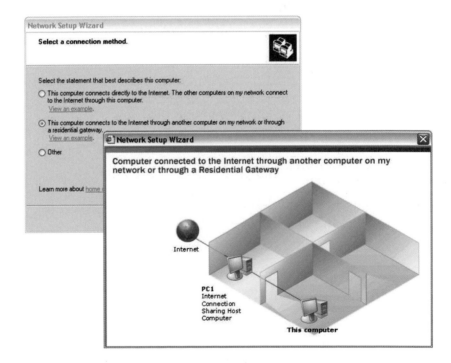

4 If your computer connects to the Internet, choose how?

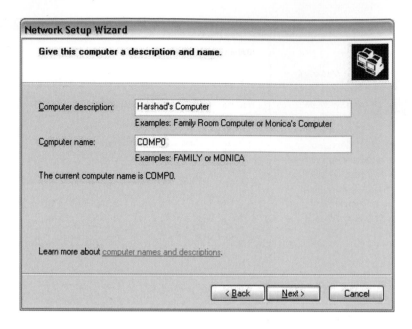

5 Specify a name and a description to identify this PC in the network. In the next dialog, the Workgroup name should be the same for all the computers in your network.

Your settings will be different to the ones shown here.

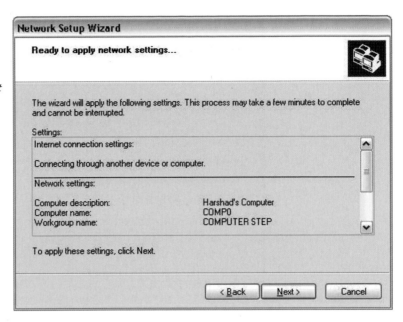

6 Check that your settings are correct. If they aren't click on the Back button and change them. Then watch the animation as your network is set up.

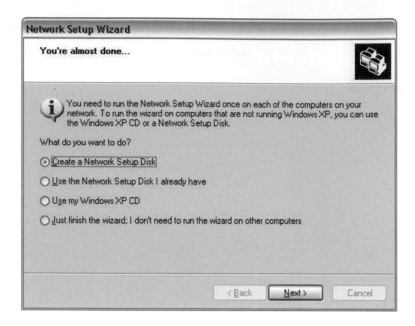

7 It's recommended that you Create a Network Setup Disk to run on other computers in your network – these can be Windows 98, ME or XP computers. Finally, click on the Finish button.

You can run the Network Setup Wizard again to change any of the settings.

My Network Places

Once your network is set up, use My Network Places to easily browse any shared information on other computers. It is very similar to My Computer (page 36) which shows local files in your own computer.

My Network Places

I Double-click on My Network Places icon from the desktop, or select it from the Start menu.

The computers with the shared folders/drives in your network must be switched on before you can access them.

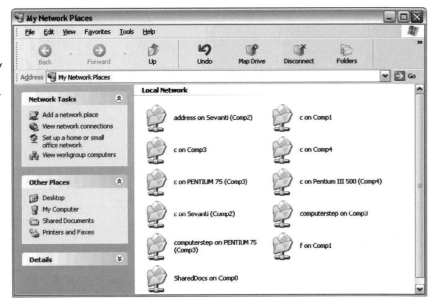

From the Workgroup computers view, double-click on a computer icon not only to see its shared folders, but also any network printers that may be attached — double-click on the printer icon to manage your print (see page 126).

2 Double-click on any shared network folder you want to access.

3 From the Network Tasks pane, click on View workgroup computers to look at all networked computers in your workgroup.

4 Also from Network Tasks, click on Add a network place to create additional paths to shared folders, a web folder on the Internet, or an FTP site. These will then also appear under My Network Places.

Sharing your Folders and Printers

The quickest and easiest way to share your files is to move them to the Shared Documents folder. This resides within My Computer. You can transfer whole folders here for everyone in your network to have access. If you're an adminstrator you can share any folder on your system as shown below. Also covered here is how to share the printer attached to your computer with other network users.

Check that there is an entry for 'File and printer sharing for Microsoft Networks' when you right-click on your Network Connection icon and select Properties.

To share a folder

Right-click on the folder you want to share. Then click on the Sharing and Security... option from the short menu.

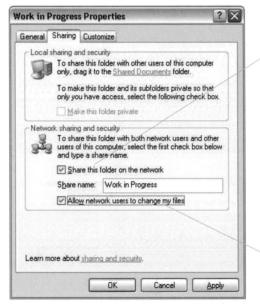

Although it's possible to share your entire hard disk drive using the method here, it is not recommended.

2 Check this box to allow sharing and choose a share name if different.

3 Check this box to allow other users to update your files. Otherwise, they'll only have read-only access.

4 A little hand appears below the folder icon to indicate that it is shared:

Work in Progress

To share your printer

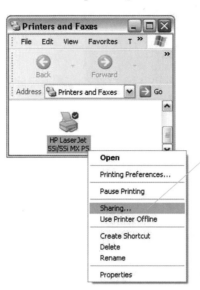

Access all your printers from the Start menu, Printers and Faxes.

Right-click on the printer you want to share, and then click on the Sharing... option.

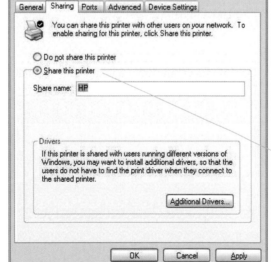

Before you can use a shared printer set up on another computer on the network, you will need to set it up again on your computer as a network printer (see page 122). Then print your documents as normal using the new network printer.

2 Select 'Share this printer' option and specify a name for all your network users.

3 A little hand appears below the printer icon.

HP LaserJet
5Si/5Si MX PS

Using Shared Resources from other Computers

Create a shortcut on your desktop to a network resource, like a folder or printer, you use frequently from My Network Places. See Creating a Shortcut, page 77.

Once a folder from another networked computer is shared (see previous topic), you can access it from My Network Places in your computer.

If you are frequently going to use the same shared folder, then it is best to assign a logical drive letter to it. Then, you can access it from My Computer in exactly the same way as any of your own physical local drives.

Logical drives don't really exist – you are mapping, say, a folder on the hard disk C in another computer to a logical drive Z on your computer. You cannot map it as the same letter C because you already use it for your own hard disk drive. You can use several letters to map different folders from one or more other computers you are connected to.

A mapped network drive appears in My Computer with a small cable at the base of the icon to distinguish it from your local drives.

Map Drive

1 Click on the Map Drive icon in the Standard Buttons toolbar from any window. If the Map Drive (and the associated Disconnect) icons aren't there, right-click on the toolbar, select Customize, and add them. You can also map onto shared drives by right-clicking on My Computer or My Network Places.

2 In the Map Network Drive dialog box the next free drive letter in descending alphabetical order is automatically allocated. Type in the shared folder path (including the computer name). e.g. \\Comp1\c

You can also right-click on a connected drive icon and select Disconnect.

Disconnect

3 Click here when you've finished using the shared drive.

Customising Windows XP

This chapter shows you how to change your Windows XP desktop and alter other settings to suit your requirements. Most of the other customisation features not included here are covered in their relevant chapters – for example, Folder Options and Customizing Folders is covered in chapter 3, Reorganising Start Menu Items is covered in chapter 5, and so on.

Covers

Chapter Ten

Appearance and Themes

You can completely change your desktop theme. This will change the colours, background wallpaper, icons, sounds, etc... to a common set theme like Underwater or Sports.

From the Start menu, select Control Panel. Then select the first option, Appearance and Themes (Category view).

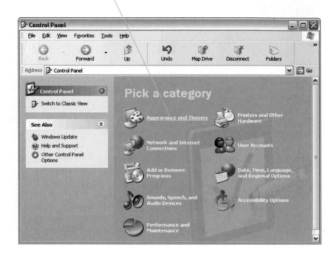

Select Change the computer's theme (or click on the Display Control Panel icon from below).

As a shortcut right-click on a clear area of the desktop and select Properties.

3 Select a theme from the drop-down list and click on Apply.

You can also browse at themes online from the drop-down list or select a theme file downloaded before.

Wallpaper, Patterns and Colours

Position drop-down choices: Center displays a wallpaper once in the centre, Tile and Stretch fill the whole desktop – either by repeating the basic design or stretching it.

Browse... locates other images to use as wallpapers – BMP, JPEG graphic files or HTML (web) pages.

Customize Desktop... (Web tab) select a web page as background.

Instead of choosing a fancy theme you can just change the desktop background by selecting that task in step 2 (or Desktop tab in Display Properties window).

Select a background image or a pattern. A pattern is a series of dots repeated. For just a plain colour desktop, first set the background to None, then pick a colour from its palette.

Screen Savers

In Settings, vary further variables of a screen saver (e.g. colours, speed, size) – the exact ones depend on the particular screen saver chosen.

Monitor Power settings are covered on page 175.

Screen savers used to prevent older monitors from burn-in when the display remained unchanged for long periods. Nowadays they're just used for fun. Select "Choose a screen saver" in step 2 page 140 (Screen Saver tab in Display Properties). Then select a Screen saver, Preview it, change the period of inactivity before it starts (Wait).

Screen Resolution

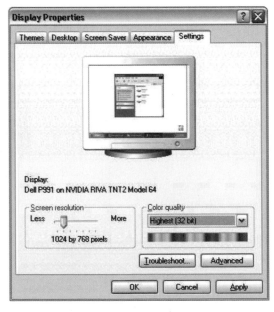

Click on the Appearance tab to customise your desktop to the way Windows use to look – Classic style.

You can also change the number of colours your monitor displays and the resolution via the Settings tab (or select it in step 2 page 140). Resolution is measured in pixels or the number of picture elements displayed. The higher this number is the sharper the picture becomes, but it also gets smaller. Adjust the Screen resolution slider as required.

User Accounts

Windows XP allows you to set up multiple users on your computer so that each user can keep their work and settings separate.

See page 21 for how to log off so another user can use your PC.

1. From the Start menu, select Control Panel. Then select User Accounts (Category view).

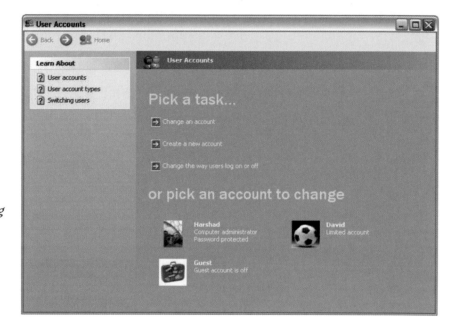

Click on "Change the way users log on or off" to enable or disable Fast User Switching – see page 11.

2. Change an account already set up or create a new one. There are three types: Computer administrator has full powers to do everything – install hardware and software, set up other user accounts, and so on; the Limited account type can use most of the programs, but can't make any major changes, and the Guest account is the most restricted so it's not even given an identity.

3. To change the picture that appears on the Welcome screen for a user, click on an account, Change my picture, Browse for more pictures and select one from My Pictures folder. You may want to replace it with a photo you've taken with a digital camera.

Date and Time

Your computer has an internal clock which may be reset at any time. It's usually displayed on the taskbar (bottom right corner) so you can keep track of time whilst working.

To display the clock

Right-click on the taskbar and select Properties, or from the Start menu go to Control Panel, Appearance and Themes category, and select Taskbar and Start menu icon.

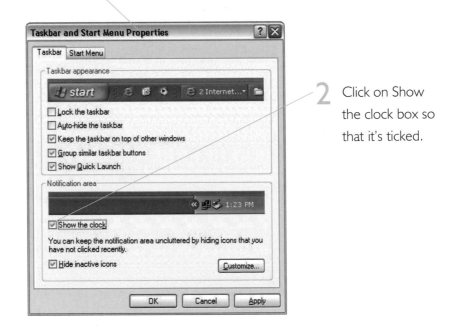

2 Click on Show the clock box so that it's ticked.

To display the date

Move your mouse pointer over the time displayed on the taskbar and leave it there for a couple of seconds. The current date then pops up.

To reset date/time

1   Right-click on the time displayed on the taskbar and select Adjust Date/Time, or from the Control Panel select "Date, Time, Language, and Regional options", Date and Time icon.

Select the Regional and Language Options icon to choose your country and formats for numbers, currency, date and time.

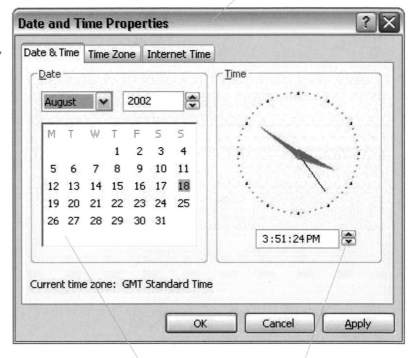

2   Click on the appropriate day from the calendar and use the arrows to change the month/ year above it.

3   Click inside the HH, MM, SS or AM/PM part of the time box and either type the new value or use the arrows.

4   Click on the Time Zone tab to change the Greenwich Mean Time to your local zone or to adjust the clock for daylight saving changes.

The time synchroniz-ation with the Internet should be immediate when you click on the Update Now button. If it fails you may not have an online connection at the time, or the date set is incorrect.

5   Click on the Internet Time tab to synchronize your clock with an Internet Time server automatically once a week.

Sounds, Speech and Audio Devices

Most PCs (especially home computers) are multimedia and therefore come pre-built with a sound card and speakers.

I Click on Start, Control Panel, "Sounds, Speech, and Audio Devices" (Category View).

Volume control

2 Select Sounds and Audio Devices icon.

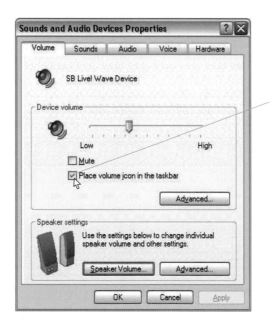

3 Ensure this check box is active and then click on Apply. A small speaker icon will appear on your taskbar.

Now, instead of turning the knob on your speakers you can adjust the volume much more easily through Windows.

If you're playing a noisy game or listening to music and the phone rings, just click on the Mute box to kill off the sound.

4 Click on the speaker icon from the taskbar and then drag the slider to adjust volume.

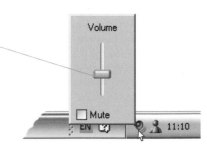

Event Sounds

You can assign different sounds to different events that occur on your PC, like when you start Windows, open a program, a contact is online in Windows Messenger, and so on.

These tabs are rarely used: Audio – for professionals wishing to select devices for sound recording and playback, Voice – if your sound card supports it you can record your own voice when playing music or online games, Hardware – lists all your multimedia devices attached and troubleshooting.

Events that have sounds associated are prefixed by the speaker icon. If you don't want any sound for a particular event, select it and then choose None in step 4.

1 Follow steps 1–2 on the previous page and then click on the Sounds tab.

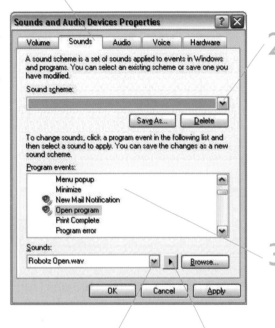

2 Select a Sound scheme from the drop-down list (e.g. Jungle, Musica, Utopia) rather than customising sounds for individual events.

3 Click on the event you want to add/ change the sound for.

4 Select a sound from the pull-down list.

5 Click to hear the sound.

Speech

On the previous page, select the Speech icon in step 2 instead. Micosoft Sam offers text-to-speech translation. Test this feature out by typing in any sample text and then clicking on the Preview Voice button to hear it.

The Taskbar

The principal components of the taskbar, usually at the bottom of the screen, are:

- the Start button (left)

- the Quick Launch toolbar (next to the Start button)

- task buttons for each open application (large area in middle)

- the notification area (right) to display the Clock, icons (Windows Messenger, Volume control, Printer etc...), the Language bar plus notification messages pop-ups

To change Taskbar properties

1 Right-click on any free space on the taskbar and then click on Properties to display the Taskbar and Start Menu Properties window as shown on page 144.

2 Click on the appropriate boxes (so that they are ticked) to turn on features, or click on ticked boxes to turn features off. For example, "Auto-hide the taskbar" will make the taskbar disappear to provide you with more desktop space. Don't worry though, you haven't lost it forever – you can still make it temporarily visible at any time by moving your mouse pointer to the screen edge.

To move/resize the Taskbar

To move the taskbar from its original bottom-of-the-screen position, drag it (from a clear area) to the top, left or right edges.

To return the taskbar to its original base, simply drag it back.

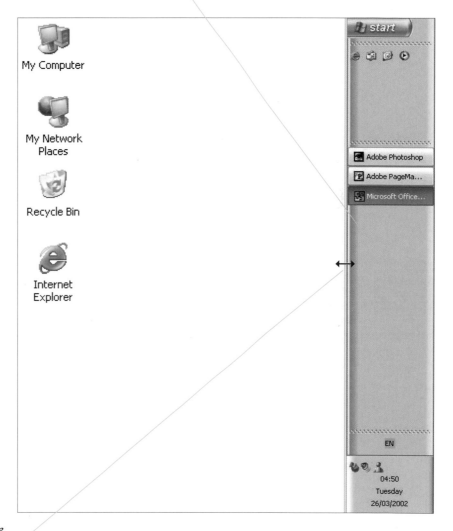

Try not to have a very wide taskbar as this will reduce your desktop space.

2 Move your mouse pointer over the inside edge of the taskbar so that it changes to a double-headed arrow. Then drag it in either direction to change the width of the taskbar.

Displaying other Toolbars on the Taskbar

2 Point to Toolbars. Then click on the relevant toolbar.

Right-click on a blank section of the taskbar.

Click here to create your own toolbars based on the contents of any folders or websites.

The Address and Links toolbars are covered in detail on pages 45-46.

The taskbar showing the Address toolbar. Drag the vertical handle to control how much of it you see

Click here to access the icons not visible

The taskbar showing the Desktop toolbar. This duplicates all the icons on your desktop, so that you can start the programs they relate to from here rather than return to your desktop. An alternative is to just click on the Show Desktop icon (usually found in the Quick Launch toolbar) to minimise all open windows, giving you a clear view of your desktop instantly.

Repositioning Toolbars

You can reposition toolbars from the taskbar to the desktop.

You can drag a toolbar to one of the desktop edges to occupy space a taskbar normally takes.

If you want to return a toolbar to the taskbar, simply drag it there, or close its window and re-display it as shown on page 150.

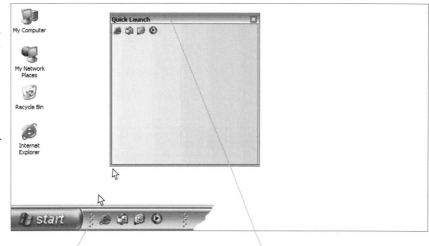

| Drag the vertical bar of a toolbar onto the desktop.

2 Release the mouse button to confirm the move.

3 If required, add additional toolbars on the desktop – right-click on an existing toolbar, point to Toolbars, and select the ones you want.

Create and then drag Windows Explorer shortcut to the Quick Launch toolbar.

Extending the Quick Launch Toolbar

You can drag any shortcuts you create on the desktop (see page 77 and the hot tip on page 79) to the Quick Launch toolbar for fast easy access.

Desktop Cleanup

In order to keep your desktop clean and uncluttered with lots of icons, there's a neat new feature in Windows XP – the Desktop Cleanup Wizard. This will remove icons from your desktop if you have not used them in the last 60 days. Don't panic though – you'll be able to retrieve them if required, from the Unused Desktop shortcuts folder created automatically on your desktop.

| Click Start, Control Panel, Appearance and Themes, Display icon. From the Desktop tab click on the Customize Desktop button.

Select or deselect these Desktop icons to enable the Cleanup Wizard to either include them or not as part of the operation.

2 Click here to run the Desktop Cleanup Wizard.

Pictures, Music and Videos

Windows XP makes it very easy to work with digital media. These include digital images from My Pictures folder, digital music from My Music folder, and digital video clips from My Videos folder. Learn how to create your own CDs, and play music or video clips on your own computer, or from the Internet, using Media Player. This chapter also introduces you to making your own home movies using Microsoft's Movie Maker.

Covers

Chapter Eleven

Capturing Pictures

Windows XP makes it easy to transfer pictures from your digital camera or scanner. Here's an example using a digital camera:

1 Plug your camera into your computer's USB port.

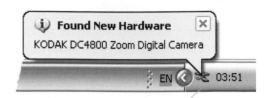

2 Windows recognises it and pops up a message in the notification area.

3 The Found New Hardware Wizard will start the first time to help you install the software for your camera from the manufacturer's CD or from the Internet.

4 A new drive letter is automatically assigned to your camera to enable you to view pictures using My Computer/ Windows Explorer in the same way as you browse at your local disk drive.

Filmstrip view is available, as shown here, when you start to browse the folder containing your pictures.

Copy selected pictures from your camera's memory to My Pictures folder or perform any other tasks from the File and Folder Tasks pane.

Working in My Pictures Folder

My Pictures folder within My Documents is the most convenient place to store, organise and work with all your images.

1 Access My Pictures folder directly from the Start menu (or from My Computer/Windows Explorer – see chapter 3).

To use one of the pictures as your desktop wallpaper, right-click on it and select Set as Desktop Background from the menu.

Thumbnails view is shown here, but you can change it from the View menu.

2 Select appropriate links from the Picture Tasks pane –

If the slideshow toolbar isn't visible, just move your mouse a little.

View as a slide show: once the slideshow starts, click to display the next slide, or use the toolbar displayed there

Order prints online: wizard allows selection of pictures and connects to the Internet to find a bureau offering a print service

Print pictures: wizard allows printing to your inkjet or other printer

Copy all items to CD: stores your pictures on a writable CD drive if you have one (see page 157)

Windows Picture and Fax Viewer

Double-click on any picture or graphic to launch the Windows Picture and Fax Viewer. The toolbar at the bottom will allow you to navigate through the images, display actual sizes of images, run a slideshow, zoom in and out of images, rotate clockwise and anti-clockwise, delete specific images, print images, save images to another folder, and edit images by opening them in your image editing program.

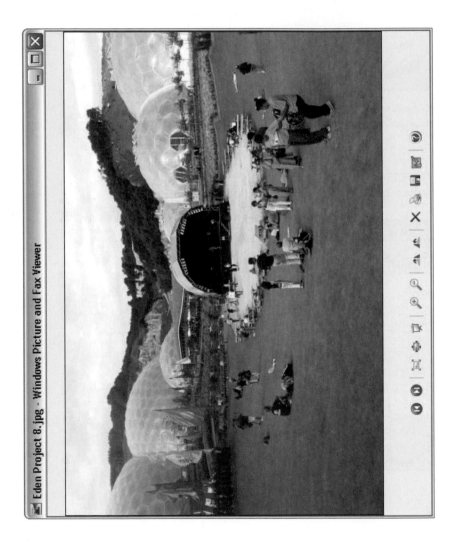

Creating your own CDs

Other ways to share your photos: email or publish to the web (select these links from the File and Folders Tasks pane).

If you have a writable CD drive, you can select and store pictures on a CD-R (Recordable Compact Disc) or a CD-RW (ReWriteable Compact Disc) to share with your friends. You can also write other media (sound, video) files, including normal text documents. The CD created can then be viewed from an ordinary CD-ROM/DVD drive. To store your pictures on a CD:

1   Select the images to copy onto a CD.

2   Click on "Copy to CD" (or if no files are selected, "Copy all items to CD" is displayed to copy the whole folder as shown on page 155) from the Picture Tasks pane.

If you're slow to click on the message balloon, access the files waiting to be written to the CD by selecting your writable CD drive from My Computer.

3   "You have files waiting to be written to the CD" message pops up, as shown on page 57. Click inside the balloon to display:

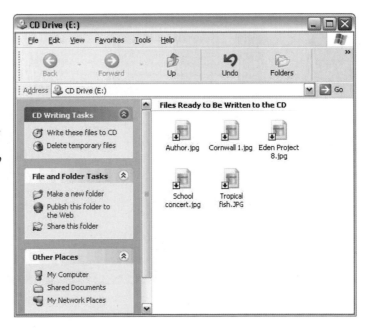

You don't have to select all the files you want to copy to a CD at the same time. Build them up over time from various folders – Windows creates a temporary area for them until you finally decide to write them to the CD.

4   Insert a blank writable CD in your drive and click on the "Write these files to CD" from the task pane.

Using Media Player

The new Media Player (v8) in Windows XP is extremely powerful and versatile – great for working with digital media. It can be used to play and create your music CDs, play Internet radio and other online media, play high-quality DVD movies, create your own playlists regardless of the source, organise all your media files, download media to a portable device like your Pocket PC or MP3 player, personalise the way it looks.

To bypass AutoPlay, press the Shift key when you insert the CD into the drive.

When you insert a CD/DVD, the AutoPlay feature in Windows starts playing whatever's on there (audio, video) in Media Player. Media Player also opens when you start playing media from the Internet. To specifically open Media Player, select it from the Start menu or click on its icon from the Quick Launch toolbar.

To play a different track simply double-click on it. Right-click on a track to disable it from playing, to move the order it's played, or to edit the name.

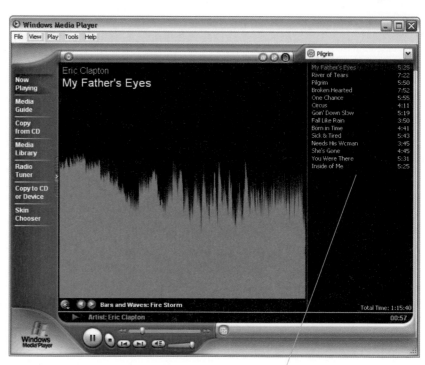

If you play the same music CD again, the track information doesn't need to be retrieved again from the Internet – Media Player stores it in your computer for quicker access.

2 If you're online, Media Player goes to the Internet and retrieves your CD's artist, title, and track information automatically.

Media Guide

When you're online the Media Guide is displayed (or click on it from the taskbar on the left to connect to the Internet). This loads the www.windowsmedia.com website, exactly same as displayed in Internet Explorer, but with the Media Player frame and buttons. From here you'll be able to play any online media.

Playlist defines a personal playing order. Create it from Media Library (covered on page 161): click on New Playlist, give it a name, say "My favourite songs". This will appear under My Playlists folder there. Now browse other folders in Media Library, right-click on links you want and choose Add to Playlist... Once completed, you can select your playlist from the drop-down list (top right) to play it.

Playlist

Control buttons when playing a CD or Internet media mimic Media bar's buttons (see page 99)

Streaming format is used to transmit radio and television shows over the Internet, and for live 'webcasts' of special events.

Most audio and video media downloaded from the Internet uses 'streaming' technology. This means that instead of downloading the whole media file (which can take a long time) before it's played, playback starts as soon as the first bit of it is downloaded. So you can start enjoying the media clip quickly whilst the rest of the file downloads in the background.

Radio Tuner

Although you can find and play Internet radio from the Media Guide covered on the previous page, it's easier to just click on the Radio Tuner task.

Select a radio station and click on the Play link to start listening. You can search for more stations on the right and when you've found an ideal one that you'd like to listen to regularly, click on the Add to My Stations link. Then, the next time you want to play the same radio station, access it from the Radio Tuner Presets list in Media Library (covered next).

Media Player Visualizations are superb – they are in sync with the music playing. You can also select specific ones from the View menu, Visualizations.

Now Playing

Click on the Now Playing task at any time to display visualizations and further details of what's being played. You'll be able to select different visualizations or Album art from just above the media playback controls.

Media Library

Media Library helps you organise and catalogue all your media into relevant folders so that you can find and play them easily from here. It works in the same way as Windows Explorer.

Click on Tools menu, Search For Media Files... to find all media files in your computer and put their links in the correct Media Library folders.

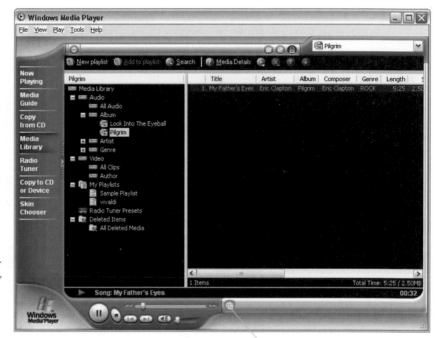

To create links in Media Library automatically when playing media from the Internet, click on Tools, Options..., Player tab and put a tick for "Add Items to Media Library when played".

Skin Chooser

Click here to switch to skin mode

Click on the Skin Chooser task and then select and apply a skin you like. Then, when you click on the Switch to skin mode button from the Media Player window, your media is played in the chosen skin instead. Double-click on the little Anchor window created to switch back to the Media Player window.

Anchor window

Skin Chooser also allows you to download more skins from the Internet for use with Media Player.

Copy from CD

Select the Copy from CD task if you want to copy tracks from your music album to your computer. Place a tick in front of the tracks to copy (uncheck the rest) and then click on Copy Music.

Your music files are copied to My Music folder by default. You can hear them from there or from Media Library.

Copy to CD or Device

This task allows you to copy media to a writable CD drive (if you have one) or to a portable media player, like the Pocket PC or MP3 player. Check the files from the left pane and select Copy Music.

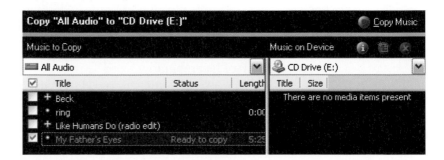

Working in *My Music* Folder

The elevation of My Pictures and My Music folders to the Start menu, alongside My Documents folder, emphasises the importance now of being able to work with digital media easily.

1   Access My Music folder directly from the Start button (or from My Computer/Windows Explorer – see chapter 3).

My Videos folder, accessed through My Computer, displays similar Video Tasks in the task pane.

You'll be able to view your music by album cover art and track information.

2   From the Music Tasks pane, select "Play All" to listen to all the music stored in My Music folder – Media Player opens automatically to play it in. Click on a folder and the "Play All" task changes to "Play selection". You can now just play the music in that folder, perhaps tracks from a specific album.

Pilgrim

3   Double-click on an album folder to display the individual tracks, then double-click on just the tracks you want to play.

01 My Father's Eyes.wma
Eric Clapton
Pilgrim

06 Circus.wma
Eric Clapton
Pilgrim

4   "Shop for music online" allows you to download and buy music from the Internet. "Copy to audio CD" task – see page 162.

Movie Maker

Windows XP includes a video editing package called Movie Maker. Just like your digital camera, it will recognise your analogue or digital video camera after you plug it in and launch Movie Maker. Now you're ready to capture and edit your video on your PC.

You'll need to have a video capture device attached to your PC.

Click on Start, All Programs, Accessories, Windows Movie Maker.

Movie Maker breaks your video footage into clips automatically.

Collections area – build up and store different video clips, sound files and still images here.

Preview area – play clips from the collection area or from the timeline below.

Once your video is constructed and saved, play it in Media Player, email clips to friends and family or publish them to a website.

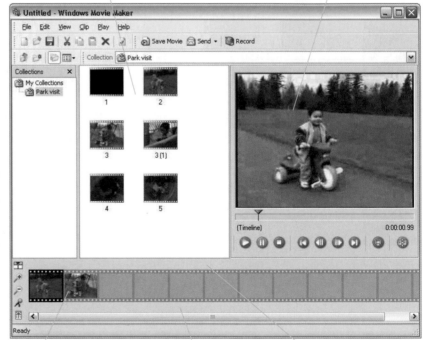

Storyboard – used to construct your film. Drag video clips, audio clips and pictures here.

Timeline – used to set how long individual clips should play for, and to fade in clips together.

Record Narration – record your voice over any part of your film.

Maintaining your System

Windows XP includes a set of tools to enhance the performance and reliability of your PC. Read this chapter to ensure you continue to work efficiently and securely.

Covers

Chapter Twelve

Displaying System Properties

System Properties displays information about your computer system and allows you to change settings for hardware, performance and automatic updates in one convenient place.

 You can also access system information and alter settings by right-clicking on My Computer icon and choosing Properties.

1 Click on Start, Control Panel (Category View), Performance and Maintenance.

2 Either click on "See basic information about your computer" task, or click on the System icon at the bottom of the window.

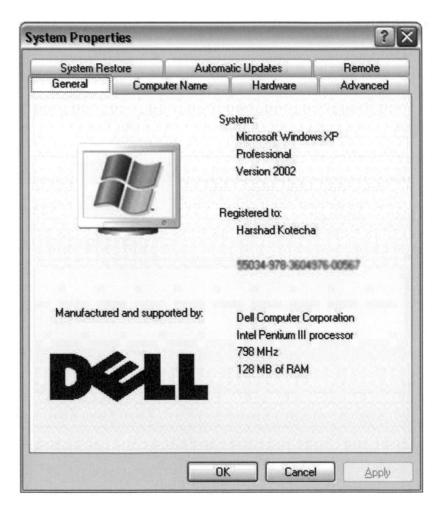

The General tab displays basic information about your computer including the version of Windows running, who it's registered to, the registration key, and the make of the computer itself.

The Computer Name tab displays your computer name and description so that it can be identified on a network. Here, you can change the name and the workgroup you want your computer to belong to.

The Hardware tab will help you install drivers through the Add Hardware Wizard. Drivers are programs required for the relevant hardware to work on your system. The Device Manager button will list all the hardware components installed on your computer – click

From the Hardware tab you can set Driver Signing options – you can ask to be warned or even block installation of drivers that have not passed Windows compatibility tests.

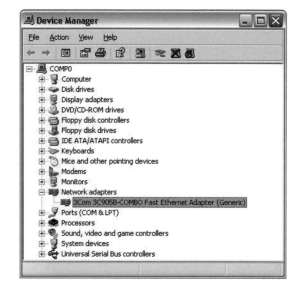

After displaying hardware properties, select the Driver tab and choose the Roll Back Driver button to switch back to the previously installed driver for that device, if the new one fails. This is a useful new feature.

on a plus sign to expand a category and then right-click on an item to change its properties. Finally, set different hardware configurations for Windows to use when it starts, if required.

The advanced tab is only used by the administrator to alter settings relating to performance including visual effects, user profiles, startup and recovery.

System Restore is covered on page 180 and Automatic updates is covered in the next topic. The Remote tab is used to setup your computer to be used from other locations.

Keeping Windows Up-to-Date

Even when you install Windows XP for the first time from a CD, if you have Internet connection, the wizard downloads the latest fixes and other updates to ensure your installation is current.

Provided you have Internet access, Windows Update can download the latest drivers, system fixes/enhancements and security updates, to ensure that your copy of Windows XP is always up-to-date.

Automatic Update

To be more efficient, set automatic updates to download new updates that apply to your system automatically in the background when you're online, and then be notified when they're ready for installation.

From System Properties (as discussed in the previous topic) select the Automatic Updates tab.

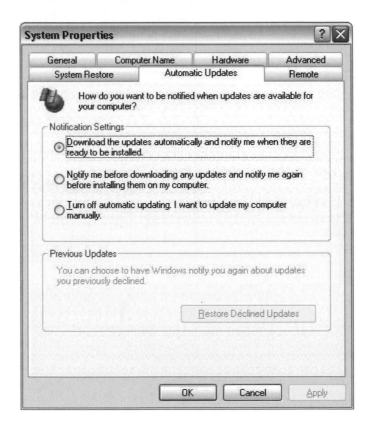

2 Select the first option as shown here and click OK.

3 You'll be informed in the notification area when new updates have been downloaded, ready for installation. Click on the message to see what the update is and install it. If it's not convenient for you to install the update right-away, because it requires you to restart your computer, for instance, click on the Remind Me Later button.

Manual Update

If automatic updates are turned off, perhaps because you have a slow Internet connection, open the Windows Update site from the Start menu. Then, Scan for updates that may apply to your system.

HOT TIP

You can also access the centralised Windows Update web site by pointing your browser to: http://windowsupdate. microsoft.com/

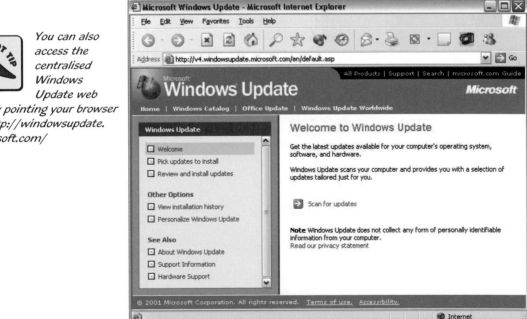

Cleaning Up your Disk

Use the Disk Cleanup utility to regain some of your disk space by removing transient files which include:

- Temporary files

- Deleted files in the Recycle Bin

- Downloaded Internet programs

Follow step 1 on page 166 and then click on "Free up space on your hard disk" task, or from the Start menu select All Programs, Accessories, System Tools, Disk Cleanup.

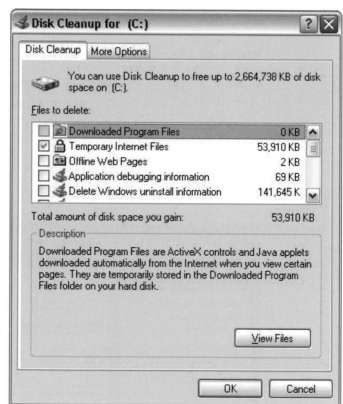

The total disk space you'll gain by deleting files in each category is shown on the right and the overall total space displayed at the top.

The View Files button will display all the files in a selected category.

2 Select one or more categories (a tick appears in the box). Then click on OK.

To save even more disk space

The first Clean up... button runs the Windows Components Wizard – see page 86. The second Clean up... button runs Add or Remove Programs – see page 84.

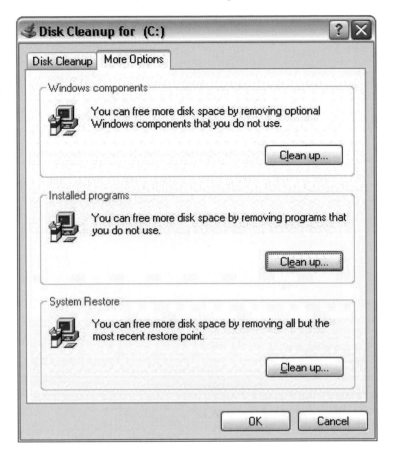

Click on the More Options tab.

2 Click on the appropriate Clean up... button(s) to remove unused Windows components, other Installed programs and space reserved by System Restore (see later) to save even more disk space.

Defragmenting your Disk

A file is not always stored in a single contiguous disk location. It may be split and stored in different areas of the disk, particularly if you frequently update and delete your files. This fragmentation doesn't damage the files, but the system takes longer to access them. This is because, at the end of each file fragment, a pointer needs to be read to give the address of where the next fragment is stored on disk. Then, the disk heads may need to move to an entirely different part of the disk to retrieve the chained fragment. This process can continue depending on how fragmented a particular file has become, making the access inefficient and slow.

You can reorganise your disk so that each file stored (perhaps as several pieces scattered all over the disk) is read and then written back in continuous storage locations. This will speed up access to all your files when you need to use them again.

Follow step 1 on page 166 and then click on "Rearrange items on your hard disk to make programs run faster" task, or from the Start menu select All Programs, Accessories, System Tools, Disk Defragmenter.

Another way to start Disk Defragmenter is to right-click on your disk, select Properties, Tools tab and then click on the Defragment Now... button.

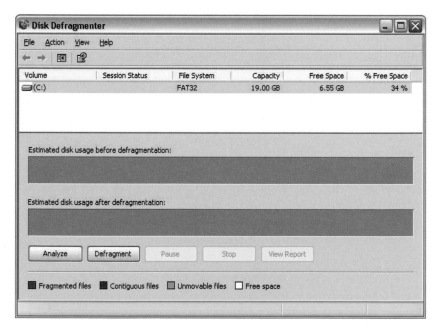

2 Select a drive and then click on the Analyze button.

3 Windows will tell you if your disk really needs to be defragmented. Click on the View Report button to see detailed analysis of how much fragmentation has occurred and a listing of the most fragmented files. You'll also be able to save or print this information.

The time it takes to defragment your hard disk will depend on:

- *how fragmented it is*
- *its size*
- *the speed of your computer*

4 Click on the Defragment button to start defragmenting your drive. A graphical colour-coded display shows the whole process working.

Click on the Pause button to temporarily hault defragmenting your drive. This will speed up other Windows programs you may be running at the same time.

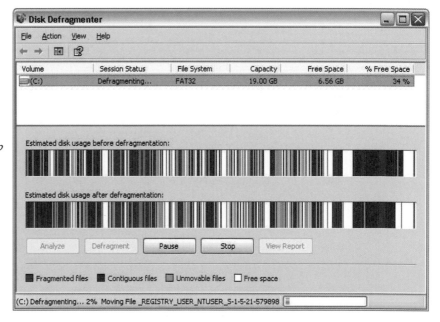

Scheduling Tasks

You can run any program automatically at the time and interval you specify, usually to schedule routine maintenance work to your system.

 You can also start from the Start button, All Programs, Accessories, System Tools, Scheduled Tasks.

1 Click on Start, Control Panel (Category View), Performance and Maintenance. Then click on the Scheduled Tasks icon.

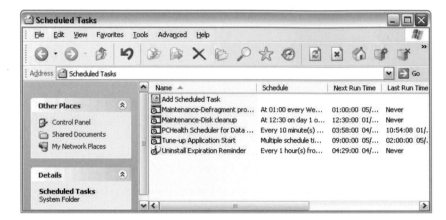

2 Double-click on the Add Scheduled Task item to run the Scheduled Task Wizard that will help you set up a new program to run at specified times.

3 After you've finished setting up a task, it appears in the Scheduled Tasks window (as above). Double-click on it to alter any of its settings. For example, the frequency it runs from the Schedule tab.

4 When you no longer want to schedule a task, simply right-click on it and select Delete to remove it from the Scheduled Tasks list.

Configuring Power Options

As long as your computer supports it you can save power by allowing Windows to:

- turn off your monitor

- turn off your hard disk

- put your PC on standby – turns off your monitor and hard disk (especially useful for portable computers)

- make it hibernate – same as standby but also saves whatever is in memory at the time to your hard disk. So when you turn your PC back on, the memory state is loaded and you can just carry on from the point you left off.

You can specify the intervals at which these shutoffs occur. You can also save these setting combinations as 'power schemes', which makes applying them even easier.

Click on Start, Control Panel (Category View), Performance and Maintenance. Then click on the Power Options icon.

It is probably more practical to use Standby or Hibernate options when required, from the Turn Off Computer button (see page 22).

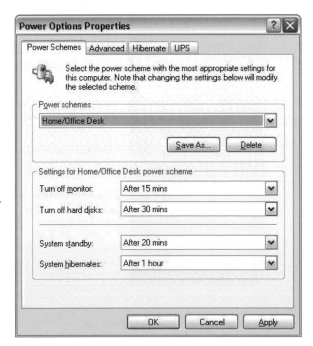

Backing Up and Restoring Data

Eventually, any hard disk drive will fail, and when it does everything stored on it is likely to be lost. Obviously, this is a very serious problem.

 For extra security, keep your backups off site, in case of major disasters like fire.

To safeguard against this problem, you should take regular backups from your hard disk. A backup is a copy of files from your hard disk to another storage medium like Zip disks, writeable CDs, a tape streamer or a Jaz cartridge.

It is recommended that you back up all the information in your computer the first time. Subsequently, say on a weekly basis, back up only the files that have changed or you've added since the previous backup.

 Another way to backup your hard disk is to right-click on it, click on Properties, Tools tab and then click on the Backup Now... button.

1 Click on Start, Control Panel (Category View), Performance and Maintenance.

2 Click on the "Back up your data" task. The Backup and Restore Wizard opens.

 You can also open this wizard from the Start button, All Programs, Accessories, System Tools, Backup.

3   Click on Next and then select if you are backing up files and settings or restoring them from a previous backup.

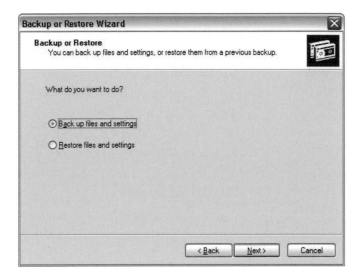

4   Next, if you selected the Backup option above, you'll need to select what you want to back up.

If you're the Computer administrator, you may want to back up all users' documents and settings.

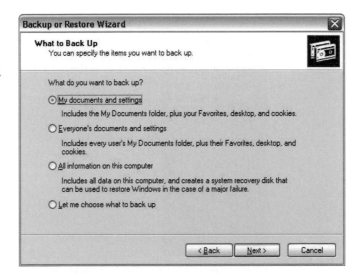

5 Next, select the destination to store your backup and type a meaningful name for the backup. You can back up to any large-capacity media like a Jaz cartridge or a tape streamer.

 Click on the Browse... button to find the path to your storage medium. It can be attached to another computer you are connected to in a network.

6 Next, the wizard confirms all your settings. If any are incorrect, click on the Back button. To start the backup, simply click Finish.

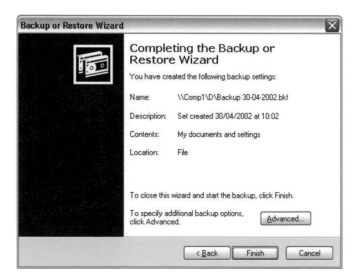

7   You can now monitor your backup progressing, including the estimated time left to complete the job, in the Backup Progress window.

Backup Progress

Drive:	C:
Label:	Backup 30-04-2002.bkf created 30/04/2002 at
Status:	Backing up files from your computer...

Progress: ▮

	Elapsed:	Estimated remaining:
Time:	1 min., 19 sec.	1 hr., 5 min.

Processing: C:\...3C}\Microsoft\Outlook Express\Inbox.dbx

	Processed:	Estimated:
Files:	14	9,306
Bytes:	19,469,614	970,621,354

You'll be able to restore files to a different drive or folder from where they originated.

8   If you ever need to restore from a backup, run the Backup program again. However in step 3, select the Restore files and settings option. The wizard will then ask you where the backup files reside before restoring them.

Using System Restore

There are essentially three types of Restore points:

- *System checkpoints – these are automatic restore points created by Windows.*

- *Manual restore points – these are the ones you'll create before a major change to your system.*

- *Installation restore points – these are created automatically when certain programs are installed.*

If things go wrong with Windows, it's very hard, even for an experienced user, to get the system working normally again. The System Restore tool resolves this problem. It monitors the changes made to Windows over time (like when you add new programs and hardware) by taking a snapshot at regular intervals of your setup. Then, if you experience problems with Windows, you can use System Restore to "roll back" to an earlier setup that did work properly.

1 Click on Start, Control Panel (Category View), Performance and Maintenance.

2 Click on the "System Restore" link in the See Also task pane.

You can also start System Restore from Start, All Programs, Accessories, System Tools, System Restore.

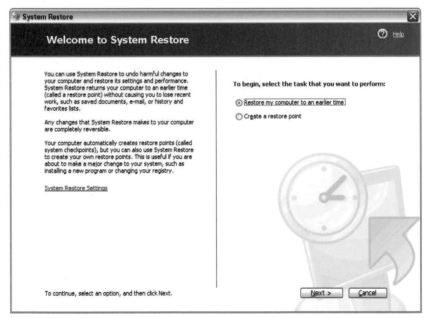

System Restore has to reserve some of your hard disk space for it to work. You can change this allocation from the System Restore tab in System Properties (see page 166).

3 Select 'Restore my computer to an earlier time' option and then click on the Next button.

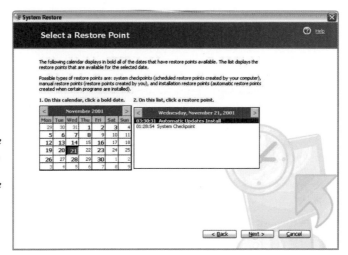

If you choose the option 'Create a restore point' in step 3, it will be marked on the calendar here as a bold date.

4 Select a bold date from the calendar (use arrows to go back and forth), and then a specific restore point. Click on Next.

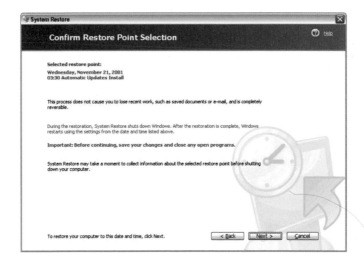

5 Ensure that all your files and programs are closed and confirm the restore point by clicking on Next.

6 Windows will display a System Restore progress bar and then restart your system.

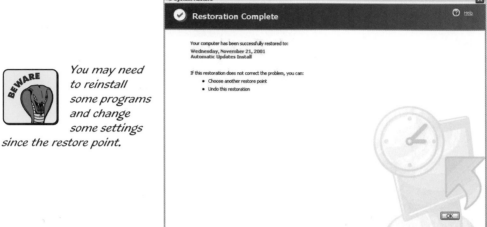

You may need to reinstall some programs and change some settings since the restore point.

7 After Windows restarts you should see a successfully restored message. Click OK.

Undoing a Restoration

Instead of Undoing a Restoration, you may decide to just restore to another point.

To begin, select the task that you want to perform:

○ Restore my computer to an earlier time

○ Create a restore point

◉ Undo my last restoration

If you've just done a restore and things haven't improved with your system, you can Undo the last restoration. Simply run System Restore again and select the option to Undo, created there automatically by Windows.

Migrating Files and Settings

A new facility in Windows XP, the Files and Settings Transfer Wizard, allows you to easily transfer files and settings from your current computer to a new one. You will now not need to worry about remembering or checking all the Windows settings you've become accustomed to and re-applying them when you buy a new computer. Some of the main settings the wizard transfers are:

- Display properties

- Folder and Taskbar options

- Internet Explorer, Outlook Express, Windows Messenger

- Mouse, Keyboard and Regional

Your applications will still need to be re-installed on your new computer.

Also your files, from My Documents, My Pictures, Shared Documents, the Fonts folder, etc... can be transferred if required.

Click on the Start menu, select All Programs, Accessories, System Tools, Files and Settings Transfer Wizard.

Files and Settings Transfer Wizard

Welcome to the Files and Settings Transfer Wizard

This wizard helps you transfer files and settings from your old computer to your new one.

You can transfer settings for Internet Explorer and Outlook Express, as well as desktop and display settings, dial-up connections, and other types of settings.

The best way to use this wizard for transferring files and settings is to use either a direct cable connection or a network. Learn more about connecting your computers.

Please close any other programs before you continue.

To continue, click Next.

< Back   Next >   Cancel

2 Click on Next and then select if this is your old computer you want to copy settings from, or the new one you want to copy settings to.

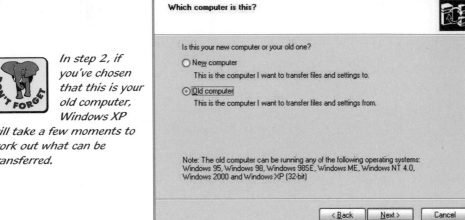

In step 2, if you've chosen that this is your old computer, Windows XP will take a few moments to work out what can be transferred.

3 Next, select the transfer method. You can choose a direct cable that connects both computers, a floppy disk or other removable media like zip/jaz/cd, or through a network drive.

4 Next, select what you want to transfer. You can transfer just the settings, files only, or both files and settings.

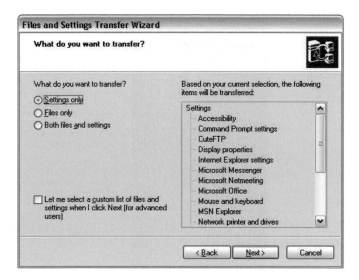

5 Next, the Collection in progress... window shows the wizard gathering the information selected for transfer and storing it at the chosen destination.

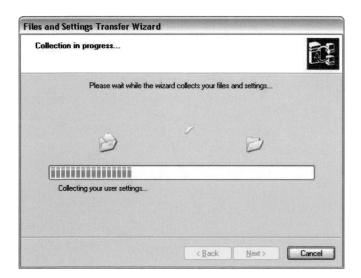

6   When all the information has been collected, the Completing the
     Collection Phase window is displayed. Click on the Finish button.

7   Now, from your new computer, run the Files and Settings Transfer
     Wizard again. However, this time select that this is your new
     computer in step 2. The wizard will prompt you to select where
     the old computer's files and settings were collected, as specified in
     step 3. Finally, the transfer will be completed.

Index

G

Greenwich Mean Time 145
Guest account 143

H

Help
  Assisted Support
    Microsoft Online Assisted Support
    (OAS) 19
    Remote Assistance 18
  Help and Support Center 14
  Index 16
  Search box. 17
Hibernate mode 22, 175
History bar 100
Home Networking. *See* Networking

I

Icons 12
  Arranging 32
  Show in Groups 32
Internet
  .NET Passport. *See* .NET Passport services
  Browsing 94
  Favorites 98
  Firewall 103
  History of websites visited 100
  Hyperlinks 93
  Internet Connection Firewall (ICF) 103

Internet Connection Sharing (ICS) 92, 131
  Media bar playback 99
  New Connection Wizard 90
  Printing web pages 101
  Radio 160
  Removing temporary files and downloaded
    programs 170
  Searching 96
    Customising the search 97
    Using a different Search Engine 97
  Time 145
Internet Explorer
  Browser buttons 95
  Image toolbar 102
  Print preview 101
  Resizing images automatically 102
  Starting 93

L

Limited account 143
Links toolbar 46
Log off 21

M

Media bar 99
Media Player 160
  Copy from CD 162
  Copy to CD or Device 162
  Media Guide 159
  Media Library 161
  Playing CDs 158
  Radio Tuner 160
  Skin Chooser 161
  Visualizations 160
Menus 24
Microsoft Sam 147